Smart Skills: Presentations

Smart Skills: Presentations

Frances Kay

Legend 🕮 Business

Independent Book Publisher

Legend Business, 107-111 Fleet Street,
London EC4A 2AB
info@legend-paperbooks.co.uk
www.legendpress.co.uk

Contents © Frances Kay 2011

The right of Frances Kay to be identified as the author of
this work has been asserted by her in accordance with the
Copyright, Designs and Patent Act 1988.

British Library Cataloguing in Publication Data available.

ISBN 978-1-78719-866-1
Set in Times

Printed in the United Kingdom by TJ International

Cover designed by:

Linnet Mattey | www.linnetmattey.com

Independent Book Publisher

Contents

Foreword

Myriads of management handbooks in print purport to provide guidance on the key skills to success and business training manuals also abound. Generally, they suffer from one or both of two defects.

Sometimes, the scope of the book is too broad. Attempting to provide comprehensive advice on all the basic business activities, there is no clear message. Nobody can gain proficiency in every field of marketing and sales, administration, purchasing, bookkeeping and financial management in a short period of time, although those who start their own businesses do need to acquire a working knowledge of most. Other titles fail to distinguish between technical capability and personal skills.

However, there are a handful of personal and interpersonal skills that are essential ingredients for success in any business: the private or public sectors and the professions; large or small organisations; employees, business owners or management consultants. These are the subject matter of the Smart Skills series on which all readers can focus to advantage because mastery of them will surely enhance both job satisfaction and their careers.

Frances Kay, herself a skilled presenter through her own work experience in workshops and talks, focuses on the essential presentation skills which are necessary in all walks of life ranging from day-to-day situations to formal occasions addressing sophisticated audiences. For want of good presentation, many a sound business concept has failed to attract funding support or in its marketing to key clients in face-to-face situations and many a promising career foundered through inability to convince colleagues and superiors. This book is both succinct and easy to follow, providing all the building bricks that you need to hone and develop your presentation skills.

In the *Smart Skills Series* Frances and her fellow authors bring together their know-how of core skills into a single compact series. Whatever your level of experience and the rung of your career ladder that you have reached, this book will help you to audit your personal effectiveness and raise your game when interacting with others.

Jonathan Reuvid

Note from Author

Public speaking and making presentations can reduce normally confident and fluent individuals to quivering jelly. And it's not easy to rise to your feet and stand on a platform in front of strangers, co-workers or superiors if you feel that your legs are unlikely to support you and your mouth won't work.

This book is designed for anyone who has to present to an audience, whether on a public speaking platform or for a specific business purpose. The principal issues for those less accustomed to speaking in public are confidence, self-belief and the ability to put across a message or idea succinctly – and convincingly. Overcoming fear of failure is the major hurdle, and it can be done – with effective training and practice.

Whether speaking and presenting in front of large public audiences, colleagues, teams, managers, sales prospects or social groups, similar principles apply. It is a question of tailoring your content and style to achieve the most favourable outcome.

The most important issues of presenting successfully are covered in this book, and among others include:

- aims for the speech or presentation;
- different audience types, sizes and disposition – and how to address them;
- time available and how best to use it in getting the message across;
- content – key points and how to deliver them;
- tips on preparation – including self-confidence, knowledge and well-being;
- speaking with or without notes, card or other prompters;
- effective use of visual aids;

- how to 'detox' your Powerpoint;
- structure, logical progression and completeness;
- managing the beginning, middle and end of your speech;
- techniques for clear, articulate delivery;
- use of words, sentences and phrases for maximum effect;
- rhetorical devices to enhance effect – metaphor, alliteration, triads;
- using your body – stance, presence, attitude, appearance, eyes, gestures, movement;
- vocal variety – pace, volume, projection, breathing;
- simple language, repetition, anecdotes, analogies.

Being able to speak effectively to an audience is something everyone should be able to do. The skills required however are rarely achieved overnight. It requires practice and regular feedback. A recommendation (by experienced presenters) is to regard the process as having three stages: before the presentation, during the event and afterwards. For the purposes of clarity that is how this book is set out.

Introduction

The opportunities – and difficulties – of getting to your feet

'The human brain is a wonderful thing. It starts working the moment you are born and never stops until you stand up to speak in public.'
Sir George Jessel

Imagine the scenario: you have been asked to give a presentation. Most of us find it difficult to resist a bit of flattery, and you feel honoured to have been singled out among your peers, so you have eagerly accepted the invitation. Then reality strikes – you'll have to stand in front of a group of people, hold their attention and address them fluently on a subject about which (someone believes) you have specialist knowledge or expertise. Let's hope you are now thinking, "That's fine. I can do it. Nothing to worry about." But what if you are having less positive thoughts?

No doubt about it, presentations matter. There can be a great deal hanging on them and rarely, if one fails to work, do you get a second chance. A poor presentation can blight a plan, a proposal, a reputation … even a career. But making a good one is not easy, as the quotation above illustrates. If you identify with this all too readily, your fears and experience will worsen if you make a presentation without understanding what's required to make it work. You will not succeed without adequate preparation and could come seriously unstuck if you believe that you can just wing it.

Many thousands of people find the idea of speaking in public utterly daunting. Some take great steps to avoid doing it, which could slow down their career progression. If you are nervous at the idea of making presentations, help is at hand. Making a good one can be done, though few people are born natural public speakers. Those that make it look easy tend to do so because they know the secret – they work at it.

Let's be honest, most of us at some time or other have to do something we don't like. This could be visiting the dentist or unblocking the kitchen sink. When faced with a task we would put off if we had the choice, the effect of delayed action simply makes the problem worse (the toothache reaches chronic levels or the unpleasant smells in the kitchen are now all over the house). What is required is a positive mind-set and an ability to rise to a new challenge.

Those of us who have had the unfortunate experience of listening to a totally unprepared speaker will have endured the consequences of things going badly wrong. People suffering from nerves stumble, hesitate and they sweat. They pepper each sentence with "ums," "ahs" and "ers". They include superfluous words, such as "basically", "actually", "'like", "well" and "you know". When asked to comment on a project, they may say "Um, er … at this moment in time we are making considerable progress with the necessary preliminary work prior to the establishment of the initial first phase of work," when they mean, "We aim to start soon".

Just when they should be impressing their audience with their expertise and confidence, and making them interested in what they have to say, they upset or confuse them. Exactly what is said and how it is put matters. As Bob Hope used to say of his early performances, "If the audience liked you, they didn't applaud, they let you live".

A common fault among inexperienced speakers is they go on too long. Often their explanations explain nothing and the direction of their speech is wholly unclear. Some presenters fidget endlessly, others remain rooted to the spot, the table or lectern held in a vice-like grip in front of them until their knuckles go white, while fear rises from them like a mist. If they use slides they can only be read from the back of the room with a telescope.

This is often made worse by their asking brightly, "Can you see alright at the back?" despite the fact that there is precious little they can do about it if the answer is "no". Worse are those who barely pause for breath as they rush headlong from one word to the next, many of them inappropriately chosen.

Of course, a lucky few believe that making a speech or presentation is easy and they can do it without rehearsal. They are convinced that they know their stuff and how to put it over. The first rule for the inappropriately overconfident is to assume that the audience is as thick as they look. Don't they realise that appearances can be deceptive? Sometimes they talk v-e-r-y s-l-o-w-l-y; use simple words and proceed on the basis that the audience has the brains of a retarded dormouse. They spell out complicated bits in CAPITAL LETTERS, speaking MORE LOUDLY as they do so.

For this kind of speaker, being on their feet is something to savour. They need only the briefest of introductions and they are away, moving quickly past the first slide without noticing that it is upside down, the coins in their trouser pocket rattling at 90 decibels and the audience hanging on their every repetitive mannerism as they mutter to themselves, "If he scratches his head whilst stood on one leg again, I'm walking out". It makes lesser mortals feel all too sadly inadequate, even the famous – it was Mark Twain who reportedly said, "It normally takes me three weeks to prepare a good impromptu speech". Poor man. Just as well he was a good writer.

Putting someone unprepared in front of any audience could be disastrous. Without an understanding of how to go about it in the right way, they will soon be in deep, deep trouble. No audience will warm to a speaker who is ill-prepared and who flounders through a speech that is tedious, confusing and poorly delivered. So, if you are not in fact a natural – and few people are – you need to give it some thought before you get to your feet. After all, once you are actually in the lion's den, you will need more survival skills than smiling and saying "Nice pussy-cat".

The way forward
Provided you are still reading and have not been put off by what has already been written, making a good speech or presentation can be exhilarating. Being able to do so is a life skill that can be an enormous asset. It can stand you in good stead in many different circumstances,

from addressing a staff meeting at work, to making a speech at a wedding or a fund raising charity event. This book is designed to act as an antidote to the problems of public speaking.

It will help you speak at work or leisure, whether you are new to the process or seeking to extend your skills. It will help calm nerves and remove the typical fear of such things as drying up, running out of time (or material) and leaving out a key point. It sets out clear, systematic guidance as to how to view the process and how to create and deliver a speech suitable to the occasion in a way that informs and impresses. It provides proven guidance that will enable you to sit down at the end of your next speech or presentation knowing that what you have put over has achieved its purpose and represents a job well done.

What follows is not just designed to help you get by, or minimise the difficulties. It will help you maximise the opportunities public speaking can give you, and make the process manageable. You won't lose your mind – only your inhibitions.

BEFORE THE PRESENTATION

Chapter One
Focusing on the task

'The first rule is to have something to say. The second rule is to control yourself when, by chance, you have two things to say. Say first one, then the other, not both at the same time.'
George Polya, Hungarian Mathematician

As mentioned in the introduction, presentations are important. For one thing, they expose you to your audience, whoever they may be. You stand up, start talking and the next few minutes can have a profound effect on whatever you are aiming to achieve. Being a good presenter can help you accomplish things and take you places.

All formal presentations (or speeches) involve an audience. It is the group that makes the difference to many people: a sea of faces, expecting ... what? Are they apprehensive? Hostile? Determined to put one over you? Before even thinking of "them", consider for a moment why presentations are so important. Their importance goes way beyond just getting a message across. It puts out all sorts of subsidiary impressions. It is the audience that influences every aspect of what must be done to make formal speaking effective. This chapter covers some important background to the detail that follows.

Once upon a time ...
Consider a typical organisation. It can be large or small. It could be

yours. On a particular day, or during a typical week, some of the items scheduled in the diaries of various executives might include:

- A presentation at a departmental meeting. Perhaps morale is a little low, there are changes to announce, belt-tightening to be instigated or new systems to be explained. The feeling may be that the group will resent or be indifferent to what must be done – yet if the reasons for the message are sound and are put over effectively then the announcement can prompt important changes and lead to improved results.
- A presentation of the annual plan for a section or division is to be made to the Board. Perhaps the hierarchy makes this difficult, perhaps the section feels it is not a major player, perhaps time to make the case and explain the details is limited – *what will they say about the budget?* Despite such feelings the whole of the next operational period will be affected by it and its success, or lack of. It must go well.
- A presentation is to be made to a major customer. A significant percentage of the annual turnover is dependent on this customer's loyalty; yet the market is increasingly competitive; product and service are being subjected to a harsh appraisal; the customer's judgement will inevitably be effected by the quality of the presentation – a good one will be interpreted as indicative of good service to come, a poor one might put the whole relationship in question, and there are eager competitors waiting on the sidelines.
- A short briefing session is scheduled to explain details of the organisation's move to new offices. The move is being made for all the right reasons, yet inevitably poses short-term problems of organising for, and coping with, the move itself. It also raises personal fears in some people as to what the new place will be like and where individuals will sit? If people co-operate enthusiastically, the move will all go more smoothly – they need to accept the move and see the advantages.

These four examples described are typical of the sort of thing that takes place in organisations everywhere, day in, day out. Such a list might include a dozen more situations: a press briefing, a training session, meetings to give advance notice of changes, to canvass support or issue instructions. It could also include significant public relations opportunities such as someone being invited to speak at a conference. Social matters may be involved: a retirement party or a welcome to a new employee, all demanding that an appropriate presentation is made.

Then there are the non-business events. You may belong to an association, chair a committee, have a daughter about to be married or a dozen other things all of which involve you rising to your feet and trying to inform and impress. All such situations involve getting things right and can have a lot hanging on them.

At a wedding, for example, the Best Man who takes their role seriously and who does their preparation will be able to enjoy watching the wedding video again and again. If they neglect thinking their speech through and attempt to do it "on the hoof"', they risk forever reaching for the fast forward button whenever the video is played.

In all these cases the importance of what is said and how it goes over – its quality – is very clear. And, even in a business context, it going well is not simply of corporate importance – it is of personal import for whoever is on their feet. Reputations will be enhanced or diluted in the process. The effect is on the outward aspect of corporate profile – and because of this your speaking ability could be called a career skill. It is something that may affect your potential to shine in your current job and work, and your capability to influence moving beyond it.

But there are also more personal implications. For the inexperienced, uninformed or untried speaker, the process is likely to be more than just difficult. It can also be literally frightening. The fact that some of the common fears are – if analysed – irrational doesn't help to dispel them. Everyone knows that the ground is *not* actually going to open up under our feet so that we sink without trace – though there may be moments, during presentations which are not going well, when we wish it would.

First steps
So, two essential points here. **The first** is that presentations are important. This may seem to be something that it is impossible to ignore (it is not; more of this later). It is certainly among the reasons why giving presentations can be so traumatic. If the idea makes you nervous, then you are among a large number of people. Most speakers, even the

most experienced, have fears to some degree. With experience comes the ability to control those fears, and minimise if not totally remove them.

Second point: presentations must go well. Let me emphasise this: *you* must *make* them go well. Short of delegation – which is not always possible even for the most senior – there is no other way.

There may be comparatively few "born speakers", but there are an increasing number of people who have learned to make a pretty good job of it. You are probably well-acquainted with someone who is living proof that presentational ability can be acquired, even by the most reluctant person. Speakers you perhaps regard as naturals almost certainly have one thing in common: they work at it. The many techniques involved (a large number are both straightforward and common sense) really do help. They help smooth and polish the presentation itself and make it psychologically easier to deal with.

An understanding of the process, and of the details of what makes it go well, what it is that achieves particular effects and how to both work at the detail and orchestrate the whole, is the foundation for good performance. Of course, practice helps too. Practice provides more experience more quickly if you understand what is going on. The scenarios referred to, and described in the introduction, highlight and contrast the skills needed and dangers when there is a lack of them.

The first step to improving whatever presentational ability you may currently have is perhaps to see it as something that *you* can change. No one is born with a readymade instant appreciation of what makes for good presentation. (A few people are, and if you were one of those you would be unlikely to be reading this). Like so much else that is worthwhile doing, some effort is required to put yourself in a position to achieve a particular standard, or to do better.

This is an on-going factor with a skill that can really always be improved – no talk is ever 100% perfect. On the other hand, working at it need not be too onerous or time-consuming. The results you can achieve from a good speech, however, make the effort in this regard well worthwhile. Before moving on to the principles that make the whole process work, two other factors are worth holding in mind.

Seeing is believing

Have you heard someone say: "what you see is what you get"? As a statement, it could be used in many contexts, but it certainly has relevance with regard to presentations. Consider by way of example someone selling a service: an accountant, designer or architect perhaps. In such professions people frequently have to make competitive presentations – sometimes called "beauty parades". It is here that potential clients make a decision as to which of a shortlist of possible service providers they will use.

If such a presentation is inexpertly done, the prospect does not think to themselves, "What an excellent designer, what a shame they cannot make a better presentation". Rather they are more likely to say, "What a rotten presentation; I bet their design work isn't very good either". In other words, additional abilities – and a wide range of them – are judged from people's competence when presenting. This may not be fair, or even reasonable, but it is without a doubt what happens.

It does not only occur in overtly sales situations (although in the example above it is particularly important because a service by its nature cannot be tested, so the impact of the people involved is critical). It occurs every time someone gets to their feet to address a group. The audience immediately begins to draw conclusions and make judgements about the person, their general proficiency and specific abilities. The perceptions that a person engenders are powerfully moulded if they have to present, much more so than in the general course of business.

The plus side of this, of course, is that good presentational standards enhance the perception of capability in other areas. By using the appropriate techniques, by putting on a professional show, you can positively and actively build your image generally. This increases the chances of acceptance for anything that you may be promoting and is true externally or internally to the organisation, as well as any group and circumstance one can think of as an audience. Anyone giving a presentation should keep this firmly in mind.

Language matters

Communication, whether one-to-one or with a group, is not easy. The aim is to make communication clear and understandable. Everybody tends to think that they can communicate. After all, we all do it all the time, especially in organisations. But in fact, without care, communication can easily deteriorate into confusion and misunderstanding. There must be hundreds of examples of communication failure despite the best intentions of the communicator. Here are some examples:

- The note left for the milkman saying: "Please deliver an extra pint today. If this note blows away, please ring bell".
- There is an old story of the journalist, researching a feature on Hollywood, sending a brief telex: "HOW OLD CARY GRANT?". In due course the message came back: "OLD CARY GRANT FINE; HOW ARE YOU?".
- There is also this wonderful phrase, usually attributed to the late ex-US President Nixon: "I know that you understand what you think I said, but I am not sure that you realise that what you heard is not what I meant".

There are many more examples, but all such stories make a point. Communication is never easy and on your feet it can be just that bit more difficult. In particular, if your tongue seems disengaged from your brain as nerves overpower precision. Many a speaker has sat down disappointed with the presentation they have just made, *knowing* they could have explained something so much better, one-to-one, or in writing, or with just a little longer to get it right. If you have done even a little presenting you do not need to be told that it is different once you are on your feet.

> 'One should not aim at being possible to understand, but at
> being impossible to misunderstand.'
> *Marcus Fabius Quintilian, Roman orator*

All this has a bearing on the audience. They *want* to understand and become restless, as well as confused, if they fail to understand the message. The audience is vital to any presenter and a number of immediate factors should be borne in mind.

- *Hearing* is not perfect. Not strictly in the medical sense, but rather because people's concentration wanders. It is just not possible to concentrate continuously (when did your attention last flit away from reading this?), but a speaker who recognises this and intentionally sets out to retain the group's interest will do better than one who ignores the fact.

- Even when people hear, the message is *diluted* as it is filtered through their existing expectations, knowledge, experience, and prejudices. The newer or more unfamiliar an idea or topic the more careful the explanation should be.
- *Conclusions* may be drawn before the full case has been put across. Once the audience has made up its mind, it is an uphill task to overturn it.

These factors can be overcome – and there is more on this later. However, at this stage a few more points are worth noting. A presenter must:

- **Look the part:** that means having an appearance which the audience associates with authority, expertise or whatever it is that is trying to be projected. It is probably unwise for the speaker to wear what they regard as comfortable or fashionable. To avoid being presumptuous in suggesting how someone should look or dress when presenting, why not think about how powerfully influenced you are by others' appearances on the speaker's platform and then act appropriately yourself.
- **Come over as a good presenter:** because, as has been said, poor presentation skills have other weaknesses read from them.
- **Be clear and interesting** so as to make a positive impact, particularly if new ideas are being proposed to the audience.
- **Show respect for the audience** in everything from being able to stick to time, to concentrating on what they will find interesting and the most appropriate way to put it across – regardless of whatever type of group you are addressing.

The audience must be kept perpetually in mind as all the various aspects of presentation are contemplated. Not only that, but a presentation that is genuinely audience-oriented will always go down better that something introspective. It may even prove easier to prepare and deliver as well.

There is perhaps one thing worse than feeling hopelessly ill-equipped to undertake the presentation and struggling to deliver it. That is to be in the audience when such an address is taking place. It is not just tedious or boring; it is embarrassing, sometimes in the extreme. Think about what that means: the audience, the group, whoever they are, *want you to succeed*.

It is easy to consider the audience as the opposition. However, with a few exceptions perhaps (for example, political situations within an organisation), they are not. They are the reason for the presentation, they want it to go well, and you can use this fact to help make it do just that.

Ideas and objectives

When preparing to make a presentation, you start work on your ideas and what you want to achieve. It is worth noting that presenting is an activity which is:

- Fragile;
- Subject to detail.

Small changes, maybe only a poorly chosen phrase, word or even emphasis, can make the difference between something going well or turning into a disaster. Similarly, small variations can boost a presentation, adding a stronger emphasis, an improved impression or real power that makes ultimate overall success more likely.

One important first rule, which affects everything about how well your presentations will come across, is simply not to attempt to wing it. Study of the subject matter and preparation for each individual presentation and consideration of the audience type makes all the difference.

- Take an interest in what makes presentations work (and fail);
- Remember that it is not a question of one single magic formula, rather of letting effective details mount up;
- Always prepare and think through what you are going to do;
- Resolve to learn from experience, your own and that of others.

Have you ever made a snap decision about something? Possibly without having had the experience? Someone has persuaded you to go to the cinema when you're not at all keen. Even before the advertisements have finished you are thinking, "I'm not going to enjoy this film". Or you are in a restaurant specialising in a type of food that is not particularly to your taste. Without having sampled a mouthful your brain is flashing the message, "This food is bound to give me indigestion." When making a presentation, audiences too can make quick and sometimes brutal judgements. Before you have said very much at all they are giving their verdict, telling themselves this will be good ... or not. Because your message needs time to make an impression, there is a good deal more to it than simply sounding or appearing pleasant.

Before embarking on the words you are going to speak, decide on how you would like to come across. Then actively focus on presenting yourself in the most appropriate way. Some factors are largely common: you will probably want to include a need to appear:

- Efficient
- Approachable
- Knowledgeable (in whatever ways the audience expects)
- Well-organised
- Reliable
- Consistent
- Confident
- Expert (and able to offer sound advice)

For example, people like to feel they are listening to someone competent, someone they can respect. Whatever the circumstances, there is a fair sized list of characteristics that are worth getting over to your audience. It will be time well spent if you think about them early on, because all of them are elements that can be *actively* added to your performance. You can *intend* to project an image of, say, confidence, and make it more than you feel. You might have to deliver a difficult (unpopular) message, in which case you will want to be seen as fair. Your persona will need to make it absolutely clear that above all this is what you are.

Anyone, whatever their role, can usefully think through the most suitable profile in this way. Before moving on, there are two important points to bear in mind:

It is not just personal
You personify your organisation and you must have a clear vision of how you want to project that too, and the department or function you are in for that matter. This is especially important when you are dealing with people with whom you have less regular or detailed contact, those in other departments for instance. Consider whether you should put over an appearance of:

- Innovation
- Long experience and substance
- Technical competence
- Having a very human face
- Confidence

Again you must decide what best suits you and your purpose. The list needs to emphasise your intended characteristics so that the total picture created is right for whoever it is to whom you are communicating. What is often required is no more than just a slight exaggeration of a characteristic, but can still be important.

Know your audience
The make up of an audience dictates how you should come across when presenting. Make yourself congruent to whoever it is you are addressing. For example, some people may have come to your presentation hoping to be entertained and amused. Others in a more formal business environment may need to hear from an experienced manager with apparent concern for his staff. If so, then any qualities creating that impression should be stressed. Others audiences may require other things. Whatever you are attempting to do, choose a style which makes sense for them.

Strategy, structure and format
Quite obviously, presentations should have a beginning, a middle and

an end. The oldest, and perhaps the wisest, saying about the nature of communications generally is the advice to: "Tell 'em, tell 'em, tell 'em". In other words, tell people what you are going to tell them, tell them, then tell them what you've told them.

It is true of a good written report that it is arranged by way of an introduction, then the body of the content, then a summary. Does this sound simple? Well, yes, it is. And it's common sense too. But it is also an area of common fault. Many otherwise good presenters dilute the impression they are making by rambling on with no clear structure. If the speaker is cobbling together random thoughts, "And I'd like to add....", "Let me just say this...." the audience will get lost and find it difficult to follow what is being said.

Audiences like to find that what is said flows logically so adopting a structured approach (the three stages: beginning, middle and end) makes it more likely that you will succeed in getting your ideas across. When preparing, keep everything organised – this will help it all to hang together logically.

But there's no point in having a structure if people are unaware of it. So this would require the need for *signposting*.

Pointing the way
The technique of *signposting* (sometimes referred to as *labelling*) is something that can be used throughout the presentation process. As long as people know broadly what they are in for, and appreciate help in keeping everything well-ordered and in context as you speak, then this technique is very important. It can literally carry the group with you. It is hard to overdo it, in fact. It consists simply of telling people, in outline or in brief, not only what is coming next but sometimes the purpose of it as well.

It is sometimes necessary to point out when you are moving on, not just in terms of topic but of stages. So you might say, "Enough by way of introduction. Let's move on to the meat of the matter. First ..."

Or, looking at the whole talk, you can spell out what is, in effect, an agenda. So if you were talking about a project of some sort, you could say: "Today I want to review three key issues. First, what needs to be done; second, who will do what; and third, the timing involved ..."

If your presentation is of any length or complexity, then a similar technique can precede and lead into sub-points. "Now, secondly, I said I would discuss the audience. Here I want to mention two main, and different, perspectives – what they expect and what they need. First of all, audience expectations ..."

Exactly the same sort of process may be relevant down several layers. One point, and something that you will need to watch, you must keep count. Should you, for instance, say authoritatively: "There are four key issues here...." When you are up to six, someone in the audience will take delight in pointing out that you don't seem to be able to count. This can be difficult to laugh off, particularly if you're presenting to a room full of accountants.

The principle of the three "tell 'ems" works not only for the overall structure, but for each individual topic – anything that is being presented in sufficient details or at such length that it needs its own beginning, middle and end. Keeping organised and letting people feel that they are following a logical structure and progression acts as a safe foundation for any presentation.

Preparing to succeed

There is one important factor regarding preparation that should be spelt out – the advantage of a systematic approach. This, for most people, is a great help. As you prepare, separate two key yet different tasks: concentrate first on the content. That is, what you will say, and only secondly move on to *how* you will put it across.

You will find that it is easier than simply looking at what you need to do sequentially. Trying to work out what you need to say and how to best put it across at the same time is difficult. It is probably quicker to prepare too – better speeches in less time seems like a good reason for going about the preparation process in a systematic way.

Avoid a sequential approach: content first, manner of delivery next, should always be the order of the day. Many details about making a presentation (described further on in this book) will reinforce the need for careful preparation. Which is why this important point is being introduced early on.

With practice the process of assembling a talk can be accomplished in a reasonable amount of time. However, to begin with, do not skimp on preparation. There is such a lot to think about, even the shortest of talks deserves care and attention.

BEFORE THE PRESENTATION

Chapter Two
Getting organised

'It usually takes me three weeks to prepare
a good impromptu speech.'
Mark Twain

Preparation is a grand word; it is also important. What it does is ensure that the brain is engaged before the mouth opens. When making presentations this is vital. It makes all the difference between a professional presentation and an indifferent one; or, at worst, an awkward and embarrassing experience. It does not just have to be done; it has to be done *thoroughly*. It has to be done right. Few personal skills come down to the application of one 'magic formula'. Life is rarely that simple. With presentations, however, preparation is crucial to success and should never be skimped.

No one wants what appears to be a well considered dramatic pause to be a wild groping for what on earth should come next. And it is difficult to concentrate on anything – still less inject some sort of flourish – when some failure of preparation is distracting you from something as basic as the next point. A systematic approach makes preparation simpler. Once you build up certain habits you will find that your preparation time is more manageable in relation to the duration of the presentation you have to make.

One point needs to be made firmly at this stage. Preparation does not mean starting at the beginning and writing out what you intend to say from beginning to end verbatim. Even if you did this, it might lead to your being tempted to read the text. That is not what presenting is about and is not likely to make for a good overall effect.

Do you watch news and current affairs programmes on TV? Have you noticed politicians reading from tele-prompters? These have a screen on which their pre-written words scroll up at just the right pace for them to read the words. They abandon all punctuation, pausing exclusively at the end of each line in a way that bears no relation to the sense of what they are saying. So, you hear something like this:

Good morning, ladies and -
Gentlemen. I am very pleased -
To be here today to speak to you -
About our policy on overseas -
Aid. This is a vital area, one that -
Contributes to Britain's role -
In …

And so on – and on; the effect is clearly not good. You should make it a rule: *do not write out your presentation in full and do not read it*.

A systematic approach to preparing your presentation is best. The starting point is to have a clear idea of your intentions and purpose.

Good intentions
Be very clear about what you are going to do (from here on it may be useful to have in mind something you do, by way of example, as you read further). Do you want to:

- Inform
- Explain or instruct
- Motivate
- Persuade
- Prompt debate
- Demonstrate
- Build on past messages or dialogue with members of the audience

You may want to do some or all of these, or to add other intentions to the list. The point here is that there may well be several things of this sort to do, and it makes preparation, and delivery, easier if you are clear about them all at the outset. You certainly do not want to be busy informing people and then suddenly think, *I really should be enthusing them a bit too*. It is difficult suddenly to try to address a newly thought of intention if you are halfway through a talk.

Purpose matters

The purpose of your talk is not what you wish to say, but what you wish to *achieve* by saying something.

For example, a manager may need to address a staff meeting of some sort about a new policy. The task is almost certainly not simply to tell them about the policy. More likely it is to ensure they understand the change and how the organisation will go about implementing it. The presentation should encourage the workforce to accept the necessity for it and be willing to adapt the way they work so it fits the new policy.

Taking a view of what needs to be done is more likely to make preparing a presentation easier and surer. Simplistically, you might break down the talk in more detail to cover five possible points:

- Some background to the change.
- An explanation of why it is necessary (perhaps in terms of the good things it will achieve).
- Exactly what the change is and how it will work.
- The effect on the individual.
- What action needs to be taken and by when.

If you think of something like a new procedure for handling customer complaints, or any sensitive or complicated issue, then the danger of some detail being omitted or inadequately dealt with (or understood) is at once clear. Given a more precise case, the purpose of your presentation should always be, as a much quoted acronym has it, SMART. That is it should be:

- **S**pecific
- **M**easurable

- **A**chievable
- **R**ealistic; and
- **T**imed

And it should have a clear focus on the audience. It is more important to think about what will work for them, rather than what it is that *you* want. To show how this works, you might regard the purpose of your reading this book as:

- Enabling you to make sure your future presentations come over in a way that will be seen by their audiences as appropriate and informative (*specific*).
- Ensuring (*measurable*) action occurs afterwards (for example, the success of the presentation might be measured by the number of people agreeing to take certain actions after they have heard you speak).
- Providing sufficient information and ideas in a manageable form so that your presentation makes a difference to what people do in future (providing an *achievable* purpose).
- Facilitating a desired result *realistically* (for example, the time it takes to read this book, while taking you away from other matters, might be compared with the possible gains from so doing).
- And *timed* (when you've read this book you will be able to review how differently you will go about making presentations in future).

Before you get up to speak you should be able to answer questions about the purpose of your presentation, such as:

- Why am I doing this? (For example, so that people are better informed.)
- What am I trying to achieve? (Say, to put them in a position to take, willingly and effectively, a particular action.)

The need for clear intentions and purpose is important. It may be more obvious in a business context, but it is just as evident for the Best Man at a wedding who has certain duties to perform. Presentations should always respect the nature of the occasion and part of their purpose should be to create a memorable occasion.

Calming the nerves
Overheard: an exchange between two speakers on a conference platform:

"Are you nervous?"
"No, I don't get nervous, I call it creative apprehension"
"Then why did you just come out of the Ladies?"

Speaking in public is often regarded as something traumatic. It can engender a particularly emotional response in many people. Some surveys regularly show it to rank high in terms of stress-inducing experiences, following closely on death and divorce. Few speakers, and this includes the most experienced, would claim to be able to make a presentation with *no* nerves. Some people say a lack of nerves is not only unlikely, it is undesirable. There is nothing like a bit of adrenalin to carry you along.

Others have vivid visions of their worst fears:

Imagine: *The previous speaker is near to concluding. You cannot seem to concentrate on what he is saying. You run over your opening remarks in your mind for the twenty-seventh time and, thus distracted, you suddenly hear the Chairman calling your name. You leap to your feet sending your notes scattering to the winds. Panic-stricken, you grovel on the floor and collect them up, half trip up the steps to the platform and take your place behind the lectern. Your rescued pages seem to sit precariously on the edge of the sloping rack, and your hands are shaking so much that you dare not try to straighten them.*

You make a start: "Good morning, Gadies and Lentlemen". Your mouth is dry and you do not seem to be able to catch your breath. You put up your first slide and it is immediately apparent that those in the rear half of the room cannot read it – though everyone notices it is upside down. Having corrected that you are pretty sure they all notice that the word "agenda" is spelt with a J.

At this point things start to go wrong.

You notice that the clock at the back of the room stopped hours ago and can offer you no guidance. The glass of water placed on your right you lightly tap with your hand, at which point it spills all over your notes. The pages stick together and you cannot leaf through them. As you attempt to separate them, the papers flutter to the floor in what looks like slow motion. Your voice dries completely; the butterflies struggle from your stomach and begin to fly around the room ...

Wake up. It is not really happening. Though mistakes do occur – I remember once driving to Bristol, arriving at the venue I was to speak at only just in time, hastening in to the room and getting out my carefully prepared notes. Standing up and starting to speak I found I had been dutifully directed by the reception staff member into the wrong conference room. No wonder everyone in the audience looked confused at what I was saying ...

So, how do you avoid all this?

Take it easy

First, be assured that it is avoidable. All, or certainly the vast majority, of these problems can be averted. Although exaggerated in the passage above, everyone commonly has some fears. In reality it is difficult to concentrate on a considered approach if you have real reservations about what lies ahead. This is only made worse if you are shaking like a leaf.

Is there a cure for nerves? Preparation is the surest way to ensure that all goes well and to minimise nerves. The key reason for nerves is the fear that something will go wrong. Prepare properly and you then *know* that a whole range of elements *will* go well.

Consider an example from the nightmare above. You need never be put out by discovering that a slide cannot be read from the back of the room if you have tried it out beforehand. You are unlikely to muddle your notes if you number the pages, less likely still if you fasten them together with a treasury tag or put them securely in some sort of file or binder.

The other helpful antidote to nerves is confidence. Confidence is a useful foundation to everything you have to do in speaking formally. Preparation – the security of knowing it is done well and thoroughly –

will help. It literally breeds confidence. This becomes a virtuous circle. Sound preparation creates confidence, more confidence makes for a better start, a good start boosts your confidence to continue, and so on ... I'm sure you get the idea.

Harnessing your secret weapons

If you've ever taken a course to help develop your presentation skills, you may have been asked by the tutor what factors make you uneasy about presenting. Be assured, *everyone* has some fears. The commonest usually include (in no particular order):

- Butterflies in the stomach;
- A dry mouth making it difficult to speak;
- Not knowing where to put your hands;
- Fear of the reaction of the audience;
- Fear of not having enough material;
- Fear of not being able to get through the material in the time;
- Not knowing how loud to pitch your voice.
- Losing your place;
- Over- or under- running on time;
- Being asked questions you cannot answer;
- Drying up.

Whether such things are real fears for you or just cause minor concern, the view to take on all this is a practical one. There are actions that actually sort out and remove some of these problems. Other issues are helped by the way you organise the speaking environment, which is explained a little further on.

So, what about the fears mentioned above?

Butterflies in the stomach: this is a physical manifestation of any worries you may have. In mild form it does no harm and fades as the adrenalin starts to flow when you get underway. On the other hand a number of practical measures undoubtedly help reduce the feeling. Some are seemingly small, perhaps obvious; they do work, however, and may work better when some are used together. They include:

- A few deep breaths just before your start;
- No heavy food too soon before you start;
- No starvation diets, or the butterflies will be accompanied by rumbles;
- No alcohol (some would say only a little) beforehand.

Plus the confidence of knowing you are well prepared and organised.

Dry mouth: again this is a natural reaction, but one simply cured. Just take a sip of water before you start. And never be afraid of asking for, or organising, a supply of water in front of you. Place it where you are least likely to spill it. Try to avoid fizzy water as it is inclined to make you burp, not desirable when you are the speaker. The longer the duration of your talk, the more you will need to take the occasional sip. Talking makes your mouth dry and an air-conditioned venue or office compounds the problem.

Somewhere to put your hands: because somehow they can seem like disproportionately large lumps at the end of your arms. The trick here is to give yourself something to do with them. You could hold a pen perhaps – and then *forget* about them. Incidentally, a man with one hand in a pocket may look all right, but both hands in pockets always appears slovenly.

Audience reaction: or rather the fear of a negative one. Ask yourself *why* they should react negatively. The fear may be irrational. It may be because you feel ill-prepared – and we have touched on preparation. Anyway, remember that audiences hate poor presentations; they *want* you to succeed.

Not having enough material: this should simply not be a fear. Your preparation will mean you *know* you have not only enough but the right amount of material for the topic and the time.

Having too much material: this needs no separate comment from the previous point, except that even if you start with too much, preparation should whittle it down to the appropriate amount.

Not knowing how loud to speak: this may be a reasonable fear in a strange room, but you can test it . Ahead of the meeting find someone to stand at the back and check how you come over, adjust your pitch until you get the level right. This is not really a very difficult problem. In other circumstances if a single person came into the room from a door at the far end, you would probably speak to them naturally at just the right level. Try not to worry and think of yourself as addressing the back row (though remember to switch off from transmit mode once you get home).

Losing your place: again there are practical measures to help, apart from knowing your message well. In particular, in terms of the exact format of the speaker's notes that you opt to have in front of you.

Misjudging the timing: in part an accurate judgement of time comes with practice. If you find it difficult do not despair. You will get better at it with experience. Timing is important, and particularly not overrunning (which is a common fault). Keeping to time is a virtue that is appreciated by many – even in the most entertaining speech. It is vital at, say, a conference when the whole day's programme can be put out by one undisciplined speaker.

Being asked questions you cannot answer: no-one is expected to be omniscient. Dealing with questions is dealt with in Chapter Seven. It is not the end of the world to say: " I don't know". An important point for any would-be presenter to accept (though you might have to make some further comment, maybe, "I'll find out and get back to you).

Drying up: here one must address the reason why this might happen. Dry mouth? Pause and have a sip of water, no one will mind. Indeed always do this if necessary. Lost your place? If that does not happen, you will not dry up. Just nerves? Well, some of the elements now mentioned – and preparation – will help. It is worth remembering here that time often seems to flow at a different rate for presenters and audiences. Often no one in the audience notices a pause, only the speaker.

In terms of attitude you should adopt a practical approach to all these sorts of feelings. Just feeling *worried* is difficult to combat. Ask yourself why you are worried. You may well surprise yourself, discovering that there is a practical solution to your fear. If so, dealing with it (as suggested above) will remove or reduce whatever factor is creating the feeling. Once done, allow yourself to put it right out of your thoughts.

Spacial awareness

This is another important area which can reduce worries – organising your environment. Don't imagine carbon footprints or Green issues. What is meant is the speaking environment: the room and, particularly, the immediate area you inhabit at the front of the room. If you work to ensure you are comfortable with all the arrangements that affect you, there is at once much less to distract your mind as you speak. You will be free to channel all your thoughts on the job in hand. If not, read on … you could be facing some of these hazards:

The table in front of you is narrow. It has an overhead projector of some sort standing firmly in its centre. There is little room for your notes and slides. There is no time to reorganise the layout, so you perch your papers on a corner of the table. You begin to place used overhead projector slides on a chair a little to one side. You are well prepared in most ways but your mind constantly flits from one hazard to the next: are your papers safe? Are you reaching far enough to put things safely on the chair? Have you remembered exactly where the curling electric wire connecting the projector to the power main lies? Why is the water jug perched on a saucer two sizes too small? And why, like so many jugs, when it pours it cascades ice cubes far and wide?

At the same time you attempt to keep small portions of your mind on the time. You maintain eye contact with members of the group and … your foot catches – just slightly – the electric cable. But it is enough to move the projector an inch or two to one side and knock the water jug …

Your own imagination can expand on this theme. Does it get better …or worse? None of this should happen. Creating the right environment needs thought and planning. Of course the precise arrangement will depend on the circumstances: such as whether there is a lectern, projector etc.

But you can and should create an arrangement as near to your ideal as any individual situation will allow. Two categories of thinking and action are necessary or desirable here:

First, prior selection and arrangement of key physical factors:

- Whether you want to use a lectern or not.
- Equipment in the right place (projector, flip chart or anything else that may be involved).
- Equipment tested and working.
- Hazards removed or taped down: as with electric wires.
- Water jug and glass standing in a safe place.
- Sufficient space for all you want to do (lay out notes, slides and so on).
- Acoustics checked (i.e. finding out how loud to speak, as mentioned).

The above factors are basic; more may occur to you and others may be necessary in special circumstances. For instance, is there a clock you can see? (if not you may want to take off your wristwatch and lay it in front of you to avoid looking visibly – pointedly – at it on your wrist.) Can you easily see any necessary signals from the Chair? Can you signal to anyone necessary (someone at the back who will summon the refreshments)?

Something else that may need organising is a microphone. It is not always necessary, but if you are using one then always test it. This has the advantage not only that the audience will be able to hear, but that you know how loud you need to speak. With modern ones you should not have to raise your voice at all, but it should accommodate a louder tone if you need this for emphasis.

The most difficult thing about fixed microphones is remembering to stay the right distance from them. The tiny radio mikes that are clipped to your lapel have a little pack which can slip inside your pocket or fasten on your belt. Once this type of mike is positioned correctly, you can just forget about it.

It may be worth making a short checklist of the things that are important to the kind of presentation you have to make and the various sorts of locations in which you may conduct them.

Note: certain things need organising differently depending on whether you are left- or right-handed. To work an overhead projector neatly, being right-handed, I need to stand to the left of it (as I face it). This is something to watch out for, especially if you are at an outside venue. Over the years of working regularly in hotels where many courses are accommodated, rarely have I been asked by the hotel staff whether I am right- or left-handed. PowerPoint operation is similarly affected.

What suits you

By this I mean not just things which you personally find create comfort for you. It doesn't matter if others are left cold by them, but what do you just *like*? What do you think of as personal comfort factors? For example, one speaker I know gives presentations regularly from behind a standard height table. It is of reasonable width with plenty of room for notes, slides, projector and more. But he always lays his notes on top of a good sized, hard briefcase, which he has placed on the table surface. Why? Because this means that his papers are just four to six inches higher so he can focus at a glance and, from the perspective of the audience, does not appear to be looking down so much. It suits him, looks fine and is easy to arrange.

Such personal "likes" can become something of a personal fetish. You *must* have certain things just right to be a 100% comfortable. Clearly if this feeling gets too strong it could become a problem. When you do not have complete control of everything, and if sometimes conditions are not ideal, you do not want this to throw you. On the other hand, perhaps if you are inclined to nerves it is actually useful to invent a few such things. Then when you organise them your way, it gives a small but useful feeling of satisfaction and you can start off feeling you are, in a sense, on familiar ground.

As a further point here, going into an unfamiliar room just before you speak is to be avoided if possible. What you have perhaps assumed is that it will be a well-equipped meeting room. It could turn out to be the very opposite and you find yourself in less than ideal circumstances and with no time to correct them. If it is your meeting, there is less of a problem (and no excuse for not checking). If you are a guest, never be afraid to raise issues in advance with the Chair or organiser. This can be done at any time – in a phone call days before the event, or face to face a few minutes before the event starts. They are normally only too happy to make some small changes if it will make you more comfortable. Be as flexible as you can and take whatever action possible to adapt to varying conditions.

BEFORE THE PRESENTATION

Chapter Three
Putting your message together

'Talking and eloquence are not the same: to speak and to
speak well are two things.'
Ben Johnson

Most, if not all, of the problems you face in speaking formally can be
removed or reduced by preparation. One of the important things (along
with your speech, equipment, visual aids) is preparing yourself. As
mentioned earlier, preparation can quite literally make the difference
between success and failure. It can also turn something ordinary into a
memorable experience. As part of the preparation process, you can "talk
yourself to success". In other words, think positively.

Psychologists say that more than 70% of what is called "self-talk"
about speaking formally is negative. This refers to all those thoughts
that start with: "I'm not sure if I can ..." or "This won't be ..." Although
this may be understandable, doubts can all too easily become a
self-fulfilling prophecy. Personal doubts that arise in this way are
intangible and not factually based. You need to combat this by thinking
positively. Imagine yourself giving the presentation and create a mental
picture of it going well. Visualise the detail of particular elements
working as you planned. Do so repeatedly and beat the negative
thoughts into submission. You could carry on the process and imagine
the applause too.

So remember all the "Ps" – Personal Preparation plus Practice makes Presenting a Positive experience for all. If you take time to address this issue, you can put self-doubt to one side.

Deciding what to say
A four-stage approach does the job of composition well, and is likely to make preparation quicker and more certain. These stages are: **listing, sorting, arranging** and **review.**

Listing
This consists of ignoring any thoughts about sequence or structure and simply listing everything – every point – that it might be desirable or necessary to say something about. You might also consider the duration and level of detail involved in order to keep things manageable. Being comprehensive is *never* one of the objectives of presenting: no audience could sit still *that* long.

This simple process gets all the elements involved down on paper. It takes just a minute or two and, for something short, might go on the back of an envelope. Alternatively, it may need more time and more than one session to complete it. What you write and how you write it down is up to you. What results could simply be a list, a column of points going down the page. Some speakers adopt a "freestyle" approach, as shown overleaf.

This freestyle approach makes it easier to encapsulate content. Rather than write a list (which tends to prompt you to think sequentially), the best starting point is to note all the possible topics/points "freestyle" around the page in a way that is free from any worry about detail such as what comes first, second and so on. This example imagines the first part of a short presentation.

How to maintain business success in difficult economic
conditions – (catchy title needed....?)

Decisions, decisions

Customer relationships

Employment
contracts

Watch your
figure(s)

New ideas

Getting paid

New prospects

Staff –
your greatest asset?

(how attractive are you?

Or your business?)

Appraisals
(are they worth it?)

Outsource to survive

Problems a small business faces

Big stick or kid gloves?
(dealing with staff)

Attitude

Thinking
laterally

Cash flow

Negotiate to win

Small is beautiful

Why delegate?

Home or away?
(to export or not)

Wow!

Mobility counts
(being flexible to change)

Doing the maths

Anger management
– for staff and customers

When this is done you can proceed to the next stage.

Sorting

Now you can start to rearrange what you have written more logically,
deciding and recording the sequence in which you will take things and
how things relate one to another. This may raise new questions as well as
resolve others, so is still not a final structure. You might simply annotate
the original list to clarify how matters will be dealt with (a second colour
is useful to do this simply). The four key actions here are to:

- Decide and note the running order.
- Link thoughts and topics that fit together.
- Delete things felt to be inappropriate or which go into too much
  detail.
- Add anything overlooked and necessary.

As you do this the amount of detail you can begin to put in will vary. It may be that you will add a good deal of detail, with some of it in the form of exact words – particularly if it is a quotation of something written or what someone has said. In other places it might be that one word is sufficient to prompt several minutes of talk.

In doing this "sorting" you need to think logically. You may also need to explain things or make points in an order that makes sense. It may be that the structure can contribute more. Could you give the whole speech a theme or a tone to make it work?

Because this overlaps with content it may be logical to do it in parallel with deciding about content. An example I have used to enliven business presentations involves telling a fairy story to help illustrate a particular situation. For example, when talking about small companies surviving the economic downturn and winning new business, you could draw on the story of *Cinderella*. The father, Baron Hardup, is the beleagured business owner. The Ugly Sisters are two bullying and difficult senior members of staff. Cinderella is the overworked and downtrodden employee, with her faithful colleague, Buttons. The Fairy Godmother is a helpful business advisor/accountant/consultant who wishes to introduce a wealthy new client to the company (Prince Charming). You get the idea ...?

This allows an amusing analogy to lead in to each section and, once you decided on something, makes preparation very much easier. By imposing a theme and arrangement, it becomes manageable. See the previous example, with annotation that might be added at this stage.

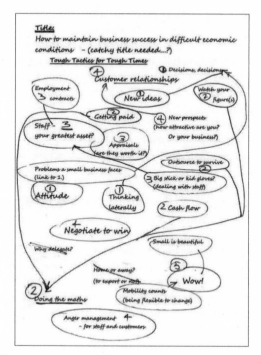

Arranging

Only now do you add (or redraft as your jottings may have become untidy and difficult to follow) the sequence and precise arrangement of the topic. Here, the general principles are shown, the detail of exactly how you should view the structure of a talk forms the thread to the next chapter. This can be simply presented – see figure overleaf – or finetuned into whatever style of "speaker's notes" works for you.

If you opt for a neat list here, then this may be the time to type it up and print it out. Such notes can begin to add a note of any emphasis necessary in presenting the material – anything from a dramatic pause to a raised voice, or a point repeated for emphasis – or this can wait until you turn your notes into actual speaker's notes suitable to have in front of you on the day.

Here we concentrate on assembling the content of the message-to-be, as it were.

Note: two points are worth a special mention here:

- Although a common fear of the inexperienced is that you will not have sufficient material, more often the reverse is true. A common fault is trying to squeeze in too much, resulting in a rushed rather that a measured delivery and an audience missing much of what is there, or worse, becoming confused.
- This limit on quantity is particularly true of individual points – there should not be too many – and the skeleton of key points, and sub-points, should stand out and be manageable within the total material.

It is difficult to suggest a rule of thumb here. It is clearly dangerous to leave out a key element of an argument, but time is at a premium for most of us these days. Clarity and brevity are both appreciated and essential. Many presenters may be given a time – "I want you to present this to the Board; just ten minutes mind". Having a clear structure allows you to be sure the content is appropriate. Then matching that to the audience and to time restraints will help you make a final decision about what you can and should include.

If in doubt it is probably better to limit points rather than confuse your audience with sheer quantity. Leaving people wanting more may be better than boring them to death with seemingly endless minute detail.

Time constraints
When time is limited this may need to be referred to specifically. In other words, as you tell people what you will do, you make it clear what is possible. In terms of the level of detail you will go into, you can explain that this is restricted by the time you have been allocated.

You do not want people to assume you have no further information to give them when in fact you have. It is far better for people to regard you as having done a good job in the time available, than thinking you should have expanded on things when that simply was not possible due to time restraints.

Now you have the rough notes of the listing and sorting stages rewritten in an ordered form, which can be subject to final review as necessary.

This then becomes the main skeleton in terms of structure and content, dividing into a beginning, middle and end, and being fleshed out and turned into your own form of running notes to provide the level of detail required.

Review

Ahead of actually setting things out in a form that works as a guide while you speak, you need to review what you have done. It is no reflection on your abilities if it is not satisfactory the first time you do this. Many people work over their material several times to get it right, though experience improves performance.

At this stage it may suffice to check over in your mind what is down on paper, though you can usefully go further and rehearse. It is possibly better advice to wait to rehearse your presentation once you have your finished "speakers notes" to hand.

This final review stage is important and can quickly finetune material into something that is not simply a sound message, but one arranged so that it can be effectively delivered.

Speaker's notes

Having prepared the presentation's content, it is now important to turn to the matter of your finished notes. What form should they take? Something clear and simple to follow is best, as it boosts confidence. Notes act like a firm hand on the tiller, assisting you to maintain direction and aiding control. They also facilitate digression – such as including anecdotes – where that may be appropriate. As has been said earlier, the trick is not to write out the speech verbatim. Better to reflect the skeleton of the material and prompt particular factors. These could be moments of emphasis, such as a dramatic pause, or using a visual of some sort. Your notes also remind you of the detail, against the background of a clear structure.

It is worth evolving a specific format that suits *you*. There is no need to follow anyone else's ideas unless you feel comfortable with them. You can always adopt what is useful from wherever you come across it. If you use the same broad approach consistently it speeds preparation. You will also quickly get to know how long a page or card in your personal style represents in terms of delivery time.

The following comments spell out a complete format suggestion in some detail. You may want to use all, or most, of this initially. You can also use – or move onto – a simplified version of it. What follows is designed to help you develop such a style. Some practical points first:

- Notes must be legible (use a sufficiently large size of typeface or writing), and legible not just as would be right sitting at your desk, but when on your feet.
- Make sure notes will stay flat as you use them on the day (a A4 ring binder may be best, or cards loosely linked with a tie-cord).
- Using only one side of the paper allows amendment and addition if necessary (or if you are using a fair number of slides then a paper copy of these might go alongside your notes).
- *Always* number the pages – you do not want to get lost (and you would not be the first to drop your notes if disaster strikes). If you prefer do the numbering in reverse, with the last page being number one, this countdown effect acts to provide information about how much material and time you have left as you proceed.
- Separate graphically different kinds of instruction and material, making clear *what* you will say and also indicating something about *how* you will say it.
- Use colour and symbols to provide emphasis.

For example, imagine first a small segment of a talk about presentations as it would be spoken in full. Here is a possible extract discussing, appropriately, speaker's notes:

Even experienced speakers worry about losing their way. What's more there are, as you may have noticed, numerous other matters you may find worrying as well. Keeping track need not be on of them.

Two main things are important here: preparation, which we have already discussed, and speaker's notes, which I will say a little about now. You need to develop a good system for creating the material you will have in front of you on the day. If you do, then doing so has real benefits. For instance, you won't lose your way. You will remember to show the next slide at the right moment and give different points the emphasis you intend. Let's see how this works.

Look at how much material you need to note down, the format that works best and how you get the key points to jump out at you as you speak.

First, how detailed do notes need to be?

And so on, but this should provide enough for our purposes.

With these actual spoken words in mind, consider what might have been down on the page to create them. This is shown (below). The detail here will be sufficient to give any speaker – who is otherwise well prepared – something easy to follow. The grey tint represents the bright colour of a highlighter pen (use your imagination!).

Certainly, colour makes a difference to the clarity of these sorts of notes and can be used in numbers of ways. If, as well as such highlighting, underlining, bullet points, certain words, symbols stand out in, say, red, it does help. In this way the eye can quickly focus on each element without too much conscious effort.

For example, the figure which charts one part of the business survival talk, uses a number of particular ideas you may be able to copy or adapt:

- The page is ruled (use colour here) into three smaller blocks that are each of a size that is easier to focus on as you look to and fro from the audience to the page (remember this example represents an A4 page, though its content could equally be spread over 2/3 cards)
- Symbols are used (for example, here to show there is a slide to put on or a need to pause). Always use the same symbol for the same thing or you may find yourself puzzling over what they mean
- Columns are used to separate main headings from the body of the notes and leave room for additional material
- Emphasis is shown (again colour does this best)
- Text is spaced out (to allow further amendment and make it easier to focus on)
- Timing is mentioned (this can repeat through the piece)
- Each page is numbered
- There are "options" that can be used, or not, as time and circumstances allow. This is something that can be very useful to both timing and fine-tuning – perhaps in light of an audiences'

reaction. The idea here is that the main content and, say, half the options will give you the duration you want. You then decide as you go along which of these to use. Such "options" can be a valuable device and injects a considerable element of flexibility into what you do; it helps you keep to time and maximise the impact you make.

Remember you should think carefully about what suits you best and evolve a personal style that works for you. It is worth a bit of trial and error to achieve this. The end result can be typed, or handwritten, or be a mixture of both.

The notes you use represent an area well worth thinking about and experimenting with. You will find that if you decide on a style of reminder note that really suits you, it will provide a real asset to you for

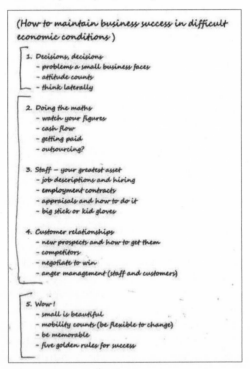

(How to maintain business success in difficult economic conditions)

1. Decisions, decisions
   - problems a small business faces
   - attitude counts
   - think laterally

2. Doing the maths
   - watch your figures
   - cash flow
   - getting paid
   - outsourcing?

3. Staff – your greatest asset
   - job descriptions and hiring
   - employment contracts
   - appraisals and how to do it
   - big stick or kid gloves

4. Customer relationships
   - new prospects and how to get them
   - competitors
   - negotiate to win
   - anger management (staff and customers)

5. Wow!
   - small is beautiful
   - mobility counts (be flexible to change)
   - be memorable
   - five golden rules for success

evermore. Your style may evolve over time, of course. You may have different versions of it for a variety of purposes.

The amount of detail you record may be different too, depending on such factors as how well you know the topic on which you must speak, or the precise duration involved. Whatever you decide, your system can always act as a sure foundation for what you have to do. Its comforting familiarity will, in time, be a valued part of its usefulness.

From first thoughts to spoken word
As an example of how the thinking can be done, let's go back to the example of the talk on small companies winning new business. At first what needs to be said may be clear only in outline:

- For any company there is more than a desire for new business.
- It is vital if the organisation is to survive.
- This can be achieved, even in the toughest economic climate.
- It just needs a realistic approach.

How is this to be explained? Next some detail is added:

- For any company there is more than a desire for new business (the pressure and stress provided by competitors, shareholders, banks etc.)
- It is vital if the organisation is to survive (no company is viable if it doesn't grow)
- This can be achieved even in the toughest economic climate (despite the gloomy predictions, there are opportunities which you may be overlooking)
- It just needs a realistic approach (you need to review your methods)

This is a factual piece and the actual content is beginning to come together, but how will it best be said? As people are often poor at winning new business and beating the competition, it needs to be made accessible. Again the initial thoughts are expanded:

- Needs a challenging start – give an example of a business which has recently won a new contract against the odds.

- If you don't win new business you'll not survive – illustration of a company losing the battle – going into liquidation/administration.
- This is achievable – tell a story to show what can be done.
- It just needs a realistic approach – suggest a way of doing something quite simple which will have an immediate positive effect (retaining existing clients costs you nothing compared to the expense of winning a new one). How good is your CRM policy?

Add an element or two to inject more life: a quotation perhaps, maybe a lighter touch, an amusing anecdote. The speaker's note will highlight the content, sequence and something of the way it is said.

Of course there is no golden rule here. How you say it must relate to a number of other factors: the nature of the audience, the duration allowed for the whole talk, and more. But the progression here is clear. Given a clear intention – here to prompt people to think about the subject and take action to improve work practices – it is easiest and most effective to start with the bare outline and add content to build towards what you want. You can then go into more or less detail as may be appropriate to match the occasion.

Rehearsal

Once you have what you aim to say planned, and documented in a form that you can refer to and speak from "on the day", you are well on the way. You may want to move from just thinking about and planning what you intend to do to actually trying it out – rehearsing. This can be done in your head, but is better if you talk through the final form out loud, or get someone to film it on your mobile phone.

Practising in front of the bathroom mirror may be less scary, but it is better (if you can face it) to have a trial run through with a sympathetic friend or colleague listening. Ask them for some constructive criticism and any ideas they may think will help, although you must ultimately decide the final form. Within an organisation you might do this on a swap basis. It takes some time, but if you have a colleague who can do it for you from time to time in return for your doing it for them it is fair and useful to both of you. For anything especially important, this is a stage well worth giving some time to. A complete run through, after all, however it may be done, is the only certain way to judge whether the duration is going to be as you want it to be.

Do not rule these ideas out because they seem embarrassing, or over the top. Even talking to a recorder in an empty room may seem odd and awkward, but rehearsal can really help, especially at a stage when your experience is still limited.

With a little help from your friends

Before moving on, there is the matter of *team presentations* to be touched on. When a complete presentation is made up of segments with perhaps two, three or more people contributing separate parts of it, the need for preparation is magnified. Team presentations must not only go over well, they must also appear *seamless*. There should be neither any disruption to the smooth flow of the content, nor any fumbling in terms of handover between speakers.

Those in the audience will read any uncertainty as unprofessional. It will seem to be either a sign of bad planning or appear as a lack of respect for the audience – or both. Even if the individual presentations are good, any fumbling on handover – "I think that's all I have to say; John, you were going to pick things up here, weren't you?" – will dilute effectiveness.

It is often extremely difficult for a group of people to present effectively without getting together beforehand to thrash out the details. Time and pressures within many an organisation may typically conspire to make such meetings difficult to arrange, but there is no substitute for them. A word or two on the telephone or a couple of e-mails is just not the same. You have been warned.

Should a group presentation be planned, you will need to consider matters such as:

- What order people will speak in (and whether this in any way should relate to the hierarchy involved; often it should not).
- Who will be "in charge".
- Who will speak first, second and so on.
- How speaking styles will match or detract.

- Who will organise and take questions.
- The implications for the timing.

There may well be more, depending on the event. It is worth a moment of your time. The effect of a seamless ultimate presentation is powerful. It is no fun getting up to speak less well prepared than you know you should be. Getting up alongside a colleague, having little idea how what the two of you say will mesh together, runs a close second.

DURING THE PRESENTATION

Chapter Four
Confronting the audience

'He speaks to Me as if I was a public meeting.'
Queen Victoria (of Mr Gladstone – one of her Prime Ministers)

As has been said earlier, the audience want it all to go well. But they are not totally forgiving and they will have expectations. Above all they want you to talk *to* them or *discuss with* them, not to talk *at* them. So keeping the audience viewpoint in mind is, like preparation, another near "magic" formula for success. It is one that should, of course, affect your preparation as well as your delivery and manner.

Any audience faced with being on the receiving end of a formal talk thinks ahead. This process may perhaps be coloured by experience of bad or boring presentations they have attended in the past. They try to guess what it will be like. They wonder if it will be interesting, amusing, or useful – or just short. Whatever the intention is, they wonder if it will be achieved. They look for clues to what it will be like even before you start.

This is why things like your appearance, starting on time, being seen to be organised and comfortable with the proceedings are all important. In training, for instance, people are asking questions such as: does this person know their subject? Will they be able to put it over? Will they do so in an interesting manner and, if they do, will it help me? Each member of a group is an individual, they are concerned above all with themselves. The good speaker appears to address individuals, not some amorphous entity called "the audience".

More specifically, the *audience wants* you to:

● "Know your stuff".
● Look the part.
● Respect them and acknowledge their situation and views.
● Make what you say link to what they want from the talk.
● Give them sufficient information to make a considered judgement about what you say (they will weigh up your views, especially if they are going to be required to take some action at the end or after you finish speaking).
● Make them understand by the time you finish what action, if any, is needed or expected of them.

Above all, they want what you say to be: *understandable, interesting* and a *good fit* with the audience and the occasion.

Conversely, *they do not want* to be:

● Confused.
● Blinded with science, technicalities or jargon.
● Lost in an overcomplicated structure (or lack of one).
● Talked down to.
● Forced to struggle to understand inappropriate language.
● Made to make an enormous jump to relate what is said to their own circumstances.

And they certainly do not want to listen to someone whose lack of preparation makes it clear that they have no respect for the group.

Any audience's attention (and certainly their respect) has to be earned. You must create a belief in your credentials for talking to them. You should build rapport between yourself and the group, make them want to listen and understand – yet perhaps also keep an open mind throughout about what is still to come. Presentation is aided by a healthy amount of empathy on the part of the speaker.

You can do a lot worse than think long and hard about any audience you are due to address. The more you know about them the better, and some prior checking is always advisable. If the group turns out to be very different, in age or experience say, from what you prepared for, there is a strong likelihood that some of what you say to them will fall on deaf ears.

You cannot overestimate the importance of a good start. Remember the old saying: *you never get a second chance to make a good first impression*. The beginning is the introduction; it must set the scene, state the topic and theme (and maybe the reason for the whole thing). Do this clearly and *then* move into the "meat" of the message, without too much delay.

Let's look at attention and rapport in turn.

Gaining attention

Two things can assist you here: your manner and the actual start you make. Your manner must get people saying to themselves: "This should be interesting – I think they know what they are talking about". Here a confident manner pays dividends. If you look the part and proceed as if you are sure of yourself then the audience will take it that you are. The assumption is made that you would not be doing the talking if you did not know your stuff. But if you appear hesitant or show any sign of being ill-prepared, hey will start to worry and that presumption will evaporate.

Exactly what you say first is also important. Not so much any formalities but the first real statement or point. What this means is that you may effectively need two starts: one that deals with any administration and formalities. Then another that is the real start into the meat of what you will say. While the first needs to be engaging and done in a way that prompts acceptance of its necessity, the second is perhaps even more important. Some examples of opening techniques you might consider using include:

- **News:** something you know they do not know (and will want to): "Gentlemen, we have hit the target. I heard just as I came into the meeting, and …"
- **Not a lot of people know...,** a startling or weird fact: "The next generation of computers, being made now in Japan, can perform ten quadrillion calculations every second". A quadrillion,

incidentally, is a number followed by 18 noughts.

The same effect might be obtained with something spoof: "There are two kinds of people in the world, those that divide people into categories, and the rest".

- **A question:** actual or rhetorical and ideally designed to get people responding (at least in their minds): "How would you like to …?"
- **A quotation:** whether famous or not. Something that generates a smile or links firmly to the topic this can work well: It was Oscar Wilde who said: "There is only one thing in the world worse than being talked about, and that is not being talked about" (used to introduce the public relations plan, perhaps).
- **A story or anecdote:** perhaps again to make a point, maybe something people know: "We all remember the moment when the …", or something they do not, "Last week in Singapore I got caught in the rain and…."
- **A fact:** preferably a striking one, or maybe challenging, provoking or surprising: "Research shows that if we give a customer cause to complain, they are likely to tell ten other people; but if we please them they will only tell one. Not a ratio to forget because…"
- **Drama:** something that surprises or shocks, or in some way delivers a punch: "The next ten minutes can change your life. It can …"
- **A gesture:** something people watch and which gets their attention: "Some people in this company seem to think that money grows on trees," – said while tearing up a bank note and scattering the pieces.
- **History:** this may be a general historical fact or one that evokes a common memory; "Five years ago, when we all knew we were at a turning point …"
- **Curiosity:** an oddity, something that will surprise and have people waiting (perhaps eagerly) for the link with what is going to be said – it may be really odd or just out of context: "Now you may wonder why I should start with a reference to pachyderms; you may even wonder what it is." (It is a thick-skinned quadruped; apparently irrelevant but …)
- **Shock:** something totally unexpected, maybe seemingly inappropriate, that really makes people listen (though its

relevance should be clear as you proceed): "Imagine this room full of dead bodies. It is a horrific thought, yet far more people than would fit in this room die every month from ..." (linked to something about charities, perhaps).

- **Silence:** this may seem a contradiction in terms, but *can* be used: "Please all remain absolutely quiet for a moment" – the speaker counts silently to ten and the gap begins to seem rather long – "that's how long it seems to customers waiting for Technical Support to answer the telephone; and it is too long..."
- **A checklist:** this can spell out what is coming and there are certainly worse starts that that: "There are four key issues I want to raise today. These are..."

This list is not exhaustive. You may have listened to presentations where the speaker used a particularly attention-grabbing introduction. Whatever device you choose, make sure it is one you are comfortable with and can deliver with confidence. You may well be able to think of several more.

Whatever you use, remember that the impact may come from several sentences rather than something as short as the examples used above. The first words, however, do need some careful thought and must be delivered in a way that achieves exactly the effect you are after.

Creating rapport

The creation of rapport is no less important than gaining interest. The two are inextricably joined. So, think of anything you can build in that will foster group feeling. For example:

- **Be careful of personal pronouns.** There are moments to say *you* and others for *we* (and sometimes fewer for *I*). Thus, "We should consider.... ", may well be better than, "You must ... Or, I think you should ..."
- **Use a (careful) compliment or two:** "As experienced people you will ..."
- **Use words that reinforce your position or competence** (not to boast, but to imply you belong to the group): " Like you, I have to travel a great deal. I know the problems it causes with continuity during an absence...".

- **Be enthusiastic**, but always genuinely so. Real enthusiasm implies sincerity and both may be needed. Expressing enthusiasm tends to automatically make you more animated, so remember another old saying: *enthusiasm is the only good thing that is infectious*.

In addition to gaining attention and creating rapport, manner and behaviour can inject additional meaning, emphasis and feeling into how you speak and thus how you come over. The factors mentioned here are varied because the process is too. No apology for that; it is the nature of the subject. Furthermore, it should be clear at the outset that the factors discussed are not mutually exclusive.

One of the complexities of this whole operation is that there is a good deal happening at one and the same time. This means that there is much to think about, indeed orchestrate at the same time. A clear understanding of the procedures involved and the development of the right reflexes and habits are really important. As you become familiar with using them it will help you to finetune your presentations on each occasion.

Everything that follows is significant because people do a lot more than just listen. They *experience* what you do. Everything about the manner and demeanour of the speaker contributes to the overall feeling people take away. And, in this, non-verbal factors are as important as verbal ones.

Think how a smile changes your view of someone. So, incidentally, smiling is something you may need to do consciously. How you look has already been mentioned; here we start, not with appearance, but with how you *look*.

Using your eyes
Eye contact with the members of the group makes an important contribution to the overall way in which a speaker is perceived. Here we review how you can maximise the impact you make in this respect. Consider first what constitutes *good* eye contact. Overall two factors are particularly important, it should be:

- **Comprehensive**, taking in all of the group (or all parts of a large audience) and continuing throughout the presentation.

- **Deliberate and noticeable** (this means that eye contact must be maintained for longer than would be normal in ordinary conversation – perhaps for periods of four to five seconds rather than two to three).

It is something that can only become truly effective once it becomes a habit but it is one that you must work to acquire. To digress for a moment: everything of this sort may seem a little daunting initially. If you can remember learning to drive, then the same feeling probably applied with that. To begin with certain aspects of the process seemed virtually physically impossible. But soon, almost without you realising it, they became habits and the whole process came together. For example, once you have had some driving experience, checking your rear-view mirror at certain points as you drive becomes all but automatic.

In presenting there are numbers of things that will acquire similar characteristics and eye contact is certainly one of them. Initially, however, you need to work at it becoming more automatic, and later at responding to it when appropriate. After all, there is no point in scanning the group if you learn nothing from it. If it appears too automatic then it will have a less positive effect on the group who, after all, want to feel you are really interested in them.

On the other hand, consider *bad* eye contact: looking too long at your notes, away from the group, looking into the corner of the room or out of the window – "What's so fascinating?" people will ask themselves. Or possibly making eye contact with one or two favoured members of the group to the exclusion of the others. Any of these can lead to you creating little or no rapport with the audience. It can mean:

- You appear anxious, nervous or, at worst, incompetent'
- You seem to lack sincerity.
- You lose the level of credibility you seek.
- You obtain little or no feedback.
- The presentation may seem to falter.
- There is no opportunity for feedback to lead to certain kinds of finetuning as the talk proceeds. For example: feedback might indicate incomprehension of some point, which can then be

elaborated (something to watch for particularly with technical points and figures).

Contrast this with *good* eye contact – which shows the speaker is in touch with the audience. It leads to a positive impression, which produces a number of benefits:

- It establishes rapport with the group, which demonstrates you care about them and increases their belief that the presentation will be right for them.
- This interest in the group increases credibility, trust and attention.
- The speaker appears more confident, more assertive, more professional, more expert (it can enhance any intended feeling of this sort).
- It allows feedback (it is useful to know if people appear attentive, interested, supportive or bored or indifferent).
- Such feedback can be used to finetune the detail of what you are doing.
- All positive benefits felt by the speaker act in some way to build confidence and this, in turn, helps improve the way in which you come over.

For example, a speaker trying to put over something difficult or contentious will find their manner (and perhaps use of feedback) contributes much to achieving their aims, or vice versa.

Watch here for, and avoid, any automatic pattern developing. It is disconcerting for an audience to see a speaker going through a routine of looking at each section of the group in, say, a regular clockwise circuit. Remember that good, natural looking eye contact is a habit to foster (and you will not develop exactly what you want perfectly or instantly). Remember too that if you are:

- well prepared;
- familiar with their material;
- working from clear notes (that do not need lengthy attention to spot what comes next);

- comfortable in your environment;
- relaxed and confident.

then your ability to produce good eye contact is enhanced.

Next we consider the most obvious speaker's resource: the voice.

Using your voice
The first step towards maximising what can be done with the voice is to be relaxed and project it effectively. The voice has an almost infinite capacity to vary meaning and emphasis. Just how something is expressed can add a great deal to its impact. Often even tiny changes in tone can vary meaning. Consider a simple sentence with the emphasis placed on particular words:

- It is your *voice* that makes the difference.
- It is *your* voice that makes the difference.

Consider too the slight difference that puts a question mark at the end of a sentence:

- You are not sure.
- You are not sure?

Now consider these two factors together:

- You are *not* sure?

So the voice needs to be used in two key ways. It must be clearly audible and it must have variety – varying pace and pitch – to produce a suitable emphasis and simply sound interesting. A dull monotone will spark no interest and prevent there being an emphasis on anything. Here we review the way in which this occurs and consider ways of achieving what you want from your voice.

It is always something of a shock to the system for people to hear their own voices, as when you record something and play it back (on video in training sessions for instance). Your voice is perhaps a particular surprise – no one *ever* hears themselves as others hear them unless they are recorded. Now everyone has a mobile phone, you can record short video clips – so you should have some idea how you sound to others. Some faults, such as talking too fast (often an effect of nerves), can quickly be corrected once people have heard how they really sound.

Two further points about the voice are important: audibility and emphasis.

Audibility

For the less experienced speaker, judging whether you will be heard clearly at the back of the room is a worry. The simplest rule is to *direct what you say at the most distant part of the room* (keep the people in the back row in mind). There is a story told of a speaker pausing to say, "Can you hear me okay at the back of the room?" They were answered by a voice saying, "Yes, but I'm prepared to swap with someone who can't". In a situation where people are struggling to hear you, the audience's view of you will change. The results of this may include the following:

● The audience tends to become irritated.
● Audience attention is less on the message than on struggling to hear.
● The speaker may well be regarded as nervous, inconsiderate, inexpert or worse.
● A low voice tends also to be monotonous and thus boring.

On the other hand, a good clear delivery has advantages that are the antithesis of the above. It gives a positive impression of the speaker as someone competent and commanding attention. In addition, speaking up tends to be one factor that helps you inject more animation and enthusiasm into a presentation. It encourages you to use gestures and generally affects the professional way in which you come over.

Emphasis

The use of the voice to inject emphasis and animation to what you do is vital. A presentation that is put over in a lively and animated tone of voice, that *sounds* interesting and which varies its pace and pitch, will always go over better than one that is delivered on some kind of monotone.

Here we review a number of seemingly simple issues that contribute to making up the total impression of your message and *how* it goes over. We start with the reverse of voice: no voice at all.

That is a ...

... pause.

What is *not* said is just as important as what is said. The pause can do a number of things:

- Allow what has just been said to sink in.
- Give time for the audience to interpret or analyse what has been said (for example, in the way that a rhetorical question can prompt thought).
- Focus attention on something other than what is said (as when using a visual aid).
- Add drama (hence the so-called "dramatic pause").
- Punctuate (making a real break to separate one point from another).

There is another benefit of the pause, one that helps you – it *gives you time to think*. This is especially important as a common fault is to speak too fast. If this is something you tend to do, it makes it all the more difficult to think as you go.

This prevents you from exercising the necessary finetuning as you progress. Regular pauses are important, even if they are no more than punctuation. You should give yourself regular opportunities to draw breath and think.

There is, however, a real difficulty with pauses – everyone thinks that they may overdo it and that the pause will then turn into an embarrassment. This is a feeling that the instigator of a pause feels much more deeply than others. The formal speaker feels it far more acutely than members of the group addressed.

This is easily demonstrated. Get someone to help you with this short experiment. Ask them to listen to you as you speak. Then, at a convenient moment, pause and count to ten slowly (to yourself). Then continue speaking. When you stop, ask them to tell you what they thought was the length of the pause. It is likely to seem longer to them. Time is relative.

If you need to pause and are worried about it becoming too long, or know you cannot judge the length you want, the solution is simple. You literally count silently to yourself (do not worry, no one will know!). In so doing you can take advantage of the fact that a pause can do a number of the things mentioned above – and add something to your presentation.

It adds variety and acts to slow any tendency for your tongue to rush away from you. Because of its importance you may find it useful to have a prompt in your notes to show where you plan to take any significant pause. This could be simply in the form of a _____.

The sound of …
How words are said is just as important as what they are. A variety of factors – the pitch of the voice, articulation, inflection, and the emphasis given to particular words or phrases (or sentences for that matter), are all instrumental in achieving your exact intended meaning. These matters are worth a separate word each:

- **Pitch:** this is the note – higher or lower – of your voice. Extremes away from the norm may add emphasis, and, of course, be coupled with other factors, for example saying something slower and lower can add a note of gravitas. This is particularly important where you want to give the impression of such factors as importance, impatience, excitement or interest. Imagine the way the strength of a negative is affected by the pitch – if it sounds too light it may be taken to mean "maybe", yet it can also be said in a way that unmistakably means NO or NO!
- **Articulation:** this is the clarity of sound you put into what you

say. If you mumble, something that is compounded by going at too fast a pace, you will not be understood. Even if you are, it is a strain for the listeners. They will not like it and may miss things as they struggle to keep up. Some things need particular clarity, for example:

– Figures (you may not want 15% mistaken for 50%).
– The sound of Fs and Ss.
– The sound at the end of words.

Before anything else, your meaning must be clear. This may well seem obvious, but still you may benefit from double-checking your clarity using a recorder.

If you sto dumble (sic), then try not to flap. We all do it and audiences understand. Take a moment, perhaps make an aside as well as pause – "Let me put my teeth back in" – and say again whatever made you stumble and was unclear. At the end of your talk it is likely that no one will even remember such a fault.

- **Inflection:** this is the way differing sound and adding an additional meaning to a phrase (in the way that there may be a clear sound that implies that a question mark follows a word). This can be important, for example a rhetorical question must be clearly recognisable as such to have its effect. This links closely to the next item below.
- **Emphasis:** this might be described as the verbal equivalent of **bold** or *italic* type.

Emphasis is always important. It is especially important in two ways to:

- Ensure that the main points shine through, and that differing elements of a presentation (main points, examples, asides and explanation, say) are clear and stand out from the whole (just as different sorts of typeface *look* different on a well set out page of print).
- Inject animation and make what is said more interesting.

The power of emphasis can be demonstrated easily. Select a word or phrase the meaning of which can be changed just by saying it with a different emphasis. These are all true examples collected over the years:

"***You're*** *coming home with me tonight*" (definite). A parent addressing a teenage daughter who is reluctant to leave a group of friends. This person has been sitting in the car getting cold for over an hour.

"*You're coming home with **me** tonight*" (incredulous). Someone attending a business event is approached by an irritating inebriated colleague who wants a lift and a bed for the night.

"*You're coming home with me **tonight**"* (seductive). Someone flirting at a party and obviously the other person is responding encouragingly.

The way you use your voice can potentially add so much to the way you present.

Next consider something at the other end of the body from where the voice emanates.

Footwork

Superficially the feet may seem to have little to do with presentation. Not so. Feet, and the stance that goes with them, are both important elements in the way a speaker both feels and thus comes over. Here therefore are some guidelines to help ensure comfort and assist in making a good impression. Note that footwork takes us into total posture and movement; other aspects of this are dealt with under the next heading (Arms and hands)..

Though it may be true that people in the audience rarely look at a presenter's feet (but you may still need to make sure your shoes are clean). Comfortable shoes which are appropriate to the occasion matter. High fashion may impress some but if by halfway through your presentation your feet are screaming, your face and voice will be affected. If you make mistakes in the way you stand the audience will pick up on this. The first question to be investigated is therefore "to move or not to move". The extremes can both cause problems:

First, *too much movement*, this:

- Can make the speaker appear nervous.
- May channel energy away from more important areas.
- May become a distraction itself.
- Could put you in the wrong place at the wrong time (out of reach of the projector or your notes).

Secondly, *too little movement*:

- Can look uncomfortable.
- Can actually be uncomfortable (you easily get stiff).
- Restricts the use of gestures and makes for a static approach.

Circumstances affect cases. You cannot move so much standing behind a lectern as you can do working from behind a table or out in the open, for instance. Always you need to find an "ideal" amount of foot movement that will both suit you and seem appropriate to the audience. As examples of the principle, such an ideal might include how you:

- Stand up straight (slouching looks slovenly – the best way of avoiding this is to imagine a string attached to the middle of the top of the head pulling straight upwards).
- Keep your feet just a little apart (shoulder width – to maintain an easy balance).
- Always move just a little to avoid cramp and add some variety.
- Move purposefully (making it clear, for example, that you are moving to be near equipment or to address a questioner more directly).

Overall a relaxed, comfortable and yet professional stance will communicate confidence (perhaps even beyond the level that is felt). The most suitable stance may vary depending on both the nature and duration of the event. Stance can make a point too: I once saw a speaker sit cross-legged on top of a table and start his speech by saying, *Not all accountants are boring*.

Arms and hands
Both arms and hands are very much more visible and noticeable to the

audience than feet; what is more they give rise to one of the most asked questions from presenters: *What do I do with my hands?* Awkwardness about what to do with them can be a distraction to the speaker. And if they *are* awkward then they become a distraction to the audience. They should be an asset to the speaker and make a positive impression on the members of the audience. They will act in this way if gestures made are appropriate and then naturally executed. Some immediate examples of use and effect will help illustrate their importance:

- Too static a pose is awkward and distracting (and may look too formal or imply nerves).
- Some static positions look protective (implying fear of the audience). This is true of standing with arms folded or clasped in front of the body.
- Too much arm waving seems nervous and is equated with fidgeting (this is especially so of arm waving and hand gestures that do not seem to relate to what is being said).

Conversely:

- A comfortable "resting" position for hands and arms is comfortable for speaker and audience alike.
- Appropriate gestures and animation add interest, enthusiasm and emphasis. They give an impression of confidence and thus expertise.

Unforeseen incidents
Here a different kind of response may be called for when there is an *accident*. You could distinguish an accident as perhaps being the speaker's fault (for example, you drop something) or the cause is far removed from the group (for instance, a fire alarm rings in a hotel meeting room). An *incident* could be as described here:

Imagine that a speaker is proceeding well. Let us say they are presenting a plan to the Board of Directors, when the meeting room door opens and a secretary or assistant enters with a tray of tea. What should the speaker do? Consider:

- Should the speaker continue?
- Will the noise (of cups and saucers being laid out) be a distraction? A serious one?
- The group is senior (the Board); would it be impolite to stop or complain?
- Was it organised for it to happen at this time?
- Could it be a mistake, perhaps the meeting should have been left undisturbed?

There is, I believe, an important rule here: *never compete with an interruption*. It will always distract and always dilute the effectiveness of what you are doing. This means that the first response to such an incident should be to acknowledge it. The *intention* must be to:

- Ensure it is clear you are not unaware of the problem (someone may well be wondering what the matter is with a speaker who carries on as if no one is distracted when clearly they are).
- Either minimise or eliminate the interruption.
- Summon assistance if appropriate.
- Maintain the overall smooth flow of the presentation as far as possible.
- Reinforce the capability of the speaker (recovering well even from minor mishaps is often well regarded, especially by those who judge they would not have done so well faced with something similar).

Consider these further by reference to our example. For instance, what options the tea delivery mentioned above might pose:

- Simply acknowledging it may remove it ("Perhaps the serving of the tea could wait just a few minutes until we are finished" – whoever is doing the delivery may, hearing this, beat a hasty retreat. In some groups, a moment's silence might well have the same effect).
- Asking the Chair (if there is one) for a view ("Would you like me to pause for a moment while the tea is laid out?" – this may prompt a number of useful responses: from agreement that you

should do so, to an instruction that the tea should wait).
- Adjust your timing so that you can break earlier than planned ("I see the tea is here. Let's break now therefore and I will pick up the point...").

Remember that it may well be necessary to complete the sentence or the point being made immediately before the event prior to interrupting to take action as described above. It may also be wise to recap a little if you break and resume later, even if the gap is slight.

Note: one regular hazard these days is the mobile phone. A reminder to turn them off is appropriate in many gatherings and the never compete with an interruption advice stands. If one rings wait until it is silenced, perhaps saying something like, "Can't be for me, mine's switched off".

Some things are so serious that there's little alternative but to stop for a while; for instance if a nothing can be heard because a helicopter is landing outside the building, or the microphone goes dead. But these are exceptions. Do not fret about the possibility throughout a talk, but bear in mind that successful recovery makes a good impression and that forewarned is forearmed.

In summary
When getting ready to confront the audience, have the following points firmly in mind.

- Describe/define the topic.
- State the purpose.
- Mention the planned duration of what you will do (not only do people like this, it also allows them to follow things better if they know when, for instance, the talk is about halfway through).
- Say why this is necessary.
- Tell them something about the structure that you plan to use.
- Say enough to catch their interest (not just for the moment, but in what is coming).
- Start, if necessary, to be seen to satisfy expectations.
- Show why what you are doing is relevant – *to them*.

- Encourage, if necessary, the audience to keep an open mind.
- Reinforce (good) early first impressions (of yourself and the event).

The manner of delivery, emphasis and so on clearly also contribute to the presentation's effectiveness. It is after all the beginning that sets the scene for the audience. They begin to judge how it is going in their terms, so if they:

- Feel it is beginning to be accurately directed at them.
- Feel their specific needs are being considered and respected.
- Feel the speaker is engaging.
- Begin to identify with what is being said – *that's right*.

Then you will have them with you and can proceed to the main segment of the presentation. You will do so with confidence because a good reaction at the start can be a firm foundation for continuing success.

DURING THE PRESENTATION

Chapter Five
Communicating your message

'Speeches are like babies – easy to conceive but hard to deliver.'
Pat O'Malley

In this chapter we look at ways of delivering your message. This is the main part of the presentation and it is doubtless also the longest. During this stage there is the greatest need for clear organisation of what you are going to say and for clarity of purpose. Your key aims here should be to:

- Put over the detail of the message.
- Maintain attention and interest.
- Do so clearly and in a manner appropriate to the audience.

Furthermore, if necessary, you may need to seek acceptance and, conversely, avoid people actively disagreeing with what you say. It is not always necessary to aim for agreement, but this is often an intention. It may well be your prime objective, especially in a work context.

Given the length and greater complexity of the middle segment, it is important for it to be well ordered. This includes the simple procedure of taking one point at a time. Here again, the following points will help this segment go well.

The main content

This needs:

- *A logical sequence:* for example discussing a process in chronological order.
- *The use of what are effectively plenty of main and sub-headings:* this is, in part, what was referred to earlier as signposting, as: "There are three key points here: performance, method and cost. Let's take performance first …" It gives advance warning of what is coming and keeps the whole message from becoming rambling and difficult to follow because of it. Imagine what you *say* rather as a report *looks*: in written form the headings stand out in bold type – your headings, the divide between sections of what you say, should be clearly audible. The longer the duration of anything you do, the more important all of this is.
- *Clarity:* people must understand what you say. There must be no verbosity. Nor too much jargon. No convoluted arguments and avoid awkward turns of phrase. This is as much a question of words as of elements of greater length. There must be no manual excavation devices – you should call a spade a spade.

Should you actually be discussing spades, they need to be relevant and interesting spades – and fit logically with your topic.

Note: To achieve prompt and clear understanding you will have to take utmost care with the words you use. Communications can be inherently difficult. Make sure that there is a considerable probability of a degree of definite cognition among those various different people in the audience: "You do understand, don't you?" Or to rephrase: you need to be sure that everyone will easily understand what you say. See this useful mnemonic:

So bear in mind such things as:

- Short words
- Short sentences
- Short paragraphs (sections)
- No more jargon that is appropriate

- Clarity of explanation
- Description that paints a picture
- Signpost intentions
- Group topics/points (groups of three to four work well; think how you remember a telephone number in short units).

Some examples here will help expand the point:

- Long words can sound pretentious: so only say *sesquipedalian* rather than *long word* if there is a very good reason.
- Certain phrases are not only convoluted, they can be annoying. Among a few that come to mind are: *at this moment in time* – when what is meant is *now*, or *in the not too distant future* – when *soon* would be better. Certainly you must avoid appearing to make things up – struggling to get something clear – as you go along: "Well, I suppose it's like … or rather, I mean …"
- The use of totally unnecessary words: *basically* at the start of a sentence or unnecessary fashionable words like everything currently being *proactive* (what is wrong with *active?*). For instance, it might well be better just to talk about a *response* rather that a *proactive* response
- Inadvertently giving a wrong impression, either by being vague: – does *quite nice* applied, say, to a person mean they are good to know or is it merely being polite? Or by being imprecise – a *continuous* process might just be continual, for instance, depending on whether it is without interval or never ending. You can doubtless think of more. In a formal situation you often do not receive much feedback or know that a false interpretation has been taken on board. You can therefore never think too carefully about exactly how you put things.
- Be descriptive with language: we might describe something as

KISS

To help understanding: Keep It Simple, Speaker

or, as some put it less politely, Keep It Simple, Stupid.

sort of shiny or, to put over a specific feeling better, as *smooth as silk*. If it is the slipperiness of it that we want to emphasise then it may need more. I heard someone on the radio recently describe something as, *as slippery as a freshly buttered ice-rink*. No one can possibly mistake that degree of slipperiness. Using similes (saying, "It is like ..." as often as you can think of good allusions) always helps paint a picture.

- Examples are also important here. It is one thing to say, "This is a change that will be straightforward and cause no problem", perhaps with the group thinking to themselves that if you expect them to believe that you will be selling them Tower Bridge next. It is quite another to say: "This is a change that will be straightforward and cause no problem," and then link it to something else: "It will be very like when the measurement system changed. There were plenty of fears about exactly what would happen, but the system and the training worked well. I don't think any of us would prefer to go back the old ways now." Though, of course, the example must be appropriate – it would be no good in the example just given if the introduction of a new system in the past was regarded as being a disaster.

- *Be careful not to make wrong assumptions:* about people's level of knowledge, understanding, degree of past experience or existing views, for instance, or what you say based on them will not hit home.

- *Use visual aids*: a picture is worth a thousand words, they say, and checklists and exhibits – and more – are all a real help in getting the message across. Let them speak for themselves (pause in speaking when you first show something – attention cannot be simultaneously on what you are saying and the visual) and make sure they *support* what you are doing rather than become the lead element – more of this in Chapter Six.

- *Include gestures:* let your physical manner add emphasis and inject appropriate feel and variety.

- *Make your voice work:* in the sense that your tone makes it clear whether you are serious, excited, enthusiastic or any other emotion or emphasis you may wish to bring to bear in this way. And watch the mechanics of the voice (speaking at the right volume and pace, for instance).

Note: a number of the above aspects, such as voice, which may appear to have been commented on only briefly here are returned to and expanded on in the next chapter.

Use words wisely

You cannot speak without using words, but what is important here is how your exact choice of words can make a real – distinct – great – considerable – powerful – pronounced – significant difference to the totality of the message that you put over. This is sufficiently important to make having a thesaurus to hand when preparing for a preparation very useful.

A poor choice of words is easy to make, perhaps compounded by any nerves you may be experiencing, and this is a common cause of presentations not being as effective as they might be. It can even be that one wrong word can switch an audience off or confuse them to a significant degree.

Sometimes the problem here is less one of incorrect thinking, and thus selection, than of not thinking at all. To clarify, the first word that comes to mind may well not be the best for the circumstances. The audience must be a major factor in your selection, dictating, for example, what degree of technicality may be appropriate, as well as a straightforward level and style of language. The dangers of too much jargon has already been mentioned, but is a sufficient hazard to deserve repeating.

You can apply exactly the same sort of thinking to phrases. For example, consider the difference in emphasis here: "Improving my presentations skills *will make me more effective in important parts of my job,*" has a much more specific meaning than: "Improving my presentations skill *will be helpful*". And if having good presentation skills will enable you to get your ideas across better and positively influence events, then why not say that?

One more point: word choice can be affected by what one might call "word-fashion". We hear words entering the language or being used in new ways all the time – language and language use is nothing if not dynamic. But words have a life cycle. Use them too early and they are misunderstood or annoy.

You will, for example, often hear on radio Americanisms, such as *upcoming events*. The more traditional *forthcoming* is just as effective but slightly old-fashioned. Use words too late in their life cycle and they are overworked and have lost their power, plus may annoy. Surely a classic example of this is the description *user friendly*. Once upon a time it was a neat, new and descriptive phrase; now every gadget in the visible universe is automatically described as user friendly – it has lost all power.

A small, but significant point that is worth noting is that a good many abbreviations do not sound right verbally. So avoid saying things like "etc." – it may be often used in print but lacks any elegance when spoken.

How you put it
As well as choosing the right words and phrases, the way in which something is said makes a difference to how it goes across. This is true in a general sense – variety, pace and so on – but also involves various specific techniques that can add to the power of what is said. For example:

- **Repetition:** Repeating a well chosen word or phrase can add emphasis. For some reason three times seems to work best. Who does not know Winston Churchill's famous speech containing the words: "We will fight them on the beaches"? The "we will fight them" phrase repeats to particularly good effect. This can work well in more mundane circumstances. You can repeat a phrase to focus on the sense of it, you can repeat a phrase to make what is said more memorable, and you can repeat a phrase in a way that builds the confidence that comes across as you speak.
- **Go quiet:** you can add power in various ways, but dropping the voice is sometimes seen as a risk and underused. This works best at the end of a point – "We must find ways of cutting costs. Our very survival depends on it and, if we do, (drops voice) *we can emerge from this period much stronger*". The final phrase said slowly and softly commands attention and makes a strong point.
- **Complexity/clarity relationship:** here a final point is thrown into sharp relief by a longer than expected run up to it – "Time is not on our side, it is already October and the year will soon be over.

What must be done before Christmas is already daunting, but _we can do this_. Let me explain why I am sure of that". The words that are underlined in the last sentence, said more slowly than the run in, and with some emphasis, can be used to make a strong point.

- **Wrong:** avoid words or phrases that someone in the audience will twitch at because they are ungrammatical or wrong in some way. So do not say: "_very unique, about 10.345%_", or talk about _future planning_ (you can plan the past? This is tautology).

Ultimately, you have to select not simply the right word or phrase, but a well selected flow of words that continue throughout the presentation. Perhaps more important than anything is clarity of meaning, linked perhaps with description which is pleasing as well as useful in conjuring up a picture.

A flourish

This is a technique which can usefully work to enhance a presentation and add an extra dimension. Here are two examples:

- This involves an appropriate "event" that is added specifically to enliven. For example, I was once in the audience at a meeting where one speaker made a dramatic start: "Ladies and Gentlemen", he began, "I know time is short, but in the hour I have available I will …" The Chairman, who sat beside him, looked horrified, tugged his sleeve and pointed to his watch. The speaker glanced in his direction for a second, and continued: "Of course, I am so sorry," he said, "In the half an hour I am allocated…" As he said this he paused, lifted his notes, in the form of A4 sheets, and tore them in half lengthways down the page, thus apparently halving the duration of his talk. He then continued – with every member of the group giving him their complete attention. The feeling in the room said, _This should be good_.

- Even so small a thing as a man removing their jacket (suggesting informality or a workshop environment) can inspire confidence. I saw this done once in two stages: first the jacket was removed, then as the presentation proceeded to complex issues he loosened his tie and rolled up his sleeves. It got a chuckle and made a point.

Such actions need an element of creativity, but you can plan their inclusion in what you do. There are, of course, dangers here. There is nothing worse than a dramatic gesture that falls flat so you need to progress with some care; I once saw someone fail to make a magic trick work. Embarrassing. The more complicated or dramatic something is, the more sure you must be that it will work.

The combining of a number of factors, both verbal and physical, to create particular impact is something that adds to the overall impression a speaker makes. When done well it is seamless. In other words, the whole thing flows smoothly along, there is variety of pace and emphasis and an occasional flourish is reached, smoothly and naturally executed, as a high point in the presentation's progress, then the flow continues. The intention is for the emphasis achieved to be more striking than the method of achieving it.

A flourish may include another factor as yet unmentioned, that of humour.

A funny thing

Humour is invaluable for varying the pace, changing the mood, providing an interval and – perhaps more important – reinforcing a point. Most talks are improved by a light moment, some speeches (at a wedding, for instance), contain an intentional and significant amount of humour.

But ... humour is a funny business and needs sensitive handling. It should not be overdone; it was Noel Coward who said: "Wit ought to be a glorious treat, like caviar; never spread it around like marmalade". This last line is applicable to illustrate just how humour can work in a presentation. It does not have to make people roll around laughing. The quote above is mildly amusing but cleverly put, and reminds me of another one: "When a thing has been said and said well, have no scruple".

Actually, quotations are useful way to inject a lighter touch to your speaking. There are many books of quotations, often focusing on particular areas from humorous ones to those that relate only to business or travel, or whatever. In addition, you may like to check out www.cyber-nation.com, a site which, apparently just because someone there likes them, lists the best part of 50,000 quotations and will let you add your favourites.

Humour is, however, difficult to judge. If you want to be sure of raising a serious smile or an outright laugh then it must be tested, or something that you know from past experience works. It is often more important for it to be successful, and pertinent, than for it to be original. Short, witty injections, of which quotes are but one example, work better in many circumstances than long stories.

The link to the topic is important. Here is an example, again it is a quote. The late Isaac Asimov, the well-known and prolific science and science fiction writer (he wrote more than 400 books), was once asked what he would do if he heard he only had six months to live. He thought for a moment, and replied in just two words: "Type faster". I quote this sometimes when giving talks about business writing and books I've written and it certainly raises a smile. More important it links well to that topic, showing the power of language, how just two words can say so much about someone, their attitudes to their work, their readers and more.

Best advice here is: use humour wisely. It is not an area on which to overstretch yourself. Always keep in mind the nature of the group, consider what you know about them and work from that.

Gaining acceptance

So far so good, but there is more to be achieved than just putting over the content. You may well want people to agree with your ideas. This can be assisted in a number of ways:

- **Relating to the specific group:** general points and arguments may not be so readily accepted as those carefully tailored to the nature and experience of a specific audience. (With some topics this is best interpreted as describing how things will affect *them* or what they will do for *them*.)
- **Provide proof:** certainly if you want to achieve acceptance, you need to offer something other than your word – as the speaker you may very well be seen as having a vested interest in your own ideas. Thus adding opinion, references or quoting test results from elsewhere and preferably from a respected and/or comparable source strengthens your case. This is evidenced by our experience in something like buying a car: are you most likely to believe the

salesman who says, "This model will do more than fifty miles per gallon" or the one who says, "Tests done by the magazine *What Car?* showed that this model does 52 miles per gallon"? Most of us will be more convinced by the latter.

It is particularly important not to forget *feedback* during this important stage:

- **Watch** for signs (nodding, fidgeting, whispered conversation, and just expressions) as to how your message is going down – try to scan the whole audience (you need in any case to maintain good eye contact around the group).
- **Listen** too for signs – a restless audience, for example, actually has its own unmistakable sound.
- **Ask** for feedback. There are certainly many presentations where asking questions of the group is perfectly acceptable and it may be expected – even a brief show of hands may assist you.
- **Aim** to build in answers to any objections that you may feel will be in the mind of members of the audience, either mentioning the fact: "I know what you are thinking: 'it can't be done in the time'. Well, I believe it can. Let me tell you how ..." Or by not making a specific mention, but simply building in information intended to remove fears.

Even if you build in answers to likely disagreement, some may still surface, so you have always to be ready to expand your proof as you go.

When you have completed the main thrust of your message then you can move towards the end.

In conclusion

Perhaps the first point to make here relates to a moment *before* the end. So be it, it is worth a mention. Good time-keeping is impressive. But it is not assumed. So flagging that the end is in sight may be useful, though you should allude reasonably specifically to what that means. If it is not just two more sentences, say so:" Right, I have two more points to make and then perhaps I may take a couple of minutes to summarise. Or, With five minutes of my time remaining, I would now like to ..."

Doing this is just signposting again, but if it engenders a feeling, which says something like: *My goodness, they look like finishing right on time*, then that can be good. Good time-keeping may be unexpected, but when it is in evidence it is always seen as a sign of professionalism.

Having said that, what are the requirements of a good ending? Two things predominate:

- A pulling together of the various points made.
- Ending on a high note.

But first, consider some dangers.

The audience can notice an ending that goes less than just right in a disproportionate way. At worst, it can spoil the whole thing. So, beware of the following:

- **False endings:** there should be one ending (preferably flagged once); if you say, ... *and finally* ... three or four times then people understandably find it irritating.
- **Wandering:** an end that never seems to actually arrive, though the nature of what is being said constantly makes it sound imminent.
- **Second speech:** a digression, particularly a lengthy one, may be inappropriate close to the end when the audience are expecting everything to be promptly wrapped up.
- **A rush to the finishing line**: this is a danger when time is pressing. It may be better to say you will overrun by a few minutes. You might consider abbreviating some of your material earlier if time is running away from you. That is preferable to gabbling the last few sentences as you race to reach the finish on time.
- **Repetition:** or at least unnecessary repetition (for effect in the summary is another matter) is something else that can distract towards the close. Repetition, or at least unnecessary repetition ... enough. Point made.

With that in mind we turn to the positive. The summary is not the easiest thing to do succinctly and accurately. When it is well done it can be impressive. Consider this in another context, that of a written report. If, after reading twenty pages, you come to three paragraphs at the end that pull the whole thing neatly together and do so effectively, then you think better of the whole document. People who find summary difficult to execute certainly respect those who do it well. So, when you are speaking (or writing reports, for that matter), this is an element of the whole that is well worth careful preparation.

A pulling together or summary is a logical conclusion, it may link to the action you hope people will take following the presentation or simply present the final point. Whatever it contains, the ending should be comparatively brief. Having made the final point – with all the other factors now referred to continuing to be important throughout this stage – you need to end with something of a flourish.

That said, it is worth mentioning that your final words should never (or at least very rarely) be, *Thank you*. It is not that a thank you is not appropriate. Indeed, it may well be essential, but it does often make for poor last words. What happens is that the talk appears to tail away, a final punchy point being apt to be followed by something like: "Well perhaps I should end with a thank you, it has been a pleasure to be here. I appreciate you giving up some of your time for this … so, many thanks to you all". It is much better to have the thank you *before* the final point: "Thank you for being here, I am grateful for your attention. Now, a final word in conclusion …" This enables your final words to be more considered and punchy.

That final word may need to be based on some simple technique (rather like the opening, so only a few examples are given here):

- **A question:** maybe repeating an opening question, maybe leaving something hanging in the air, maybe with the intention of prolonging the time people continue to think about the topic and what you have said.
- **A quotation:** particularly the sort that encapsulates a thought briefly.
- **A story:** allowing more time to put over, and emphasise, a concluding point.
- **An injunction** to act: where appropriate: "So, go out and…"

Having a clear link to what was said at the beginning works well. This may relate to content: "At the start I posed three questions, now let me see what the answers are …" Or it may be just a phrase: "I used the words 'impossible task' at the start, but is what we are considering here an impossible task? I have tried to suggest otherwise …" The neatness of such a technique seems to appeal.

However you finish, remember that your last remarks will linger in the mind a little longer than much of what went before. If you want to make people think, then your final words are a large part of what allows you to succeed in that aim.

Note: one point here that you need to bear in mind throughout the whole structure: remember that, while the beginning is important, the overall nature of what you say must remain good throughout the time you speak. It can sometimes be a trap to put good stuff first and then find that the quality tails away somewhat as you go on.

At the end your talk, when you sit down, or later back in your office or home, perhaps with a large, well earned treat, what do you want? For the audience to:

- Have had their expectations met (perhaps, better still, surpassed).
- Have understood everything that was said.
- Have followed the detail, logic and technicality of any argument you have been promoting.
- Warmed to you as a speaker (and felt whatever you may have wished to project, for example, trust or belief in your expertise, was projected).
- Seen what was done and how it was done as appropriate to them.

You might want to add to this list, wanting people to have found the whole thing interesting, stimulating, entertaining, whatever … any adjectives you choose need to reflect your circumstances and intention.

You may not feel, at this stage, that you will ever look forward to formally speaking on your feet. But you are certainly likely to arrive at the point of enjoying the relief of having *made* one. When that presentation has also gone as you wished, and you find that it has produced real satisfaction for the audience, you should congratulate yourself. If you follow all the advice here and become more confident and proficient at the process, you may begin to draw some real pleasure from it.

Can you hear me at the back?

An essential part of getting your message across concerns your voice. There is some advice in Chapter Four about its importance. But it is vital to making a good presentation, so here is a bit more on the topic. A lot of people worry about how to project. Public speaking should not be a strain. If it is then it will show; the audience will hear the strain and may even read it wrongly. They could assume you are uncertain, perhaps just when you want to sound authoritative.

Should you feel your voice is a potential problem, that it is inadequate to the task, this is rarely so. Most people have a voice that will almost certainly do the job supremely well. Have you ever listened to children in a playground? They all have huge voices and seemingly endless lung capacity. Projecting their voice causes them no problem at all. (If you live near a school, you will know this.)

Why should that ability change with age? If it does then it is because the wrong habits build up. The solution is relaxation and breathing.

Some years ago I attended a training course at RADA to help improve my public speaking and presenting skills. The course tutor gave us the following good advice regarding voice:

Most people do not breathe properly when they speak. The breath supports the voice and has plenty of power and energy. If you speak on the "held" breath, this creates tension and stress in the voice and blocks off the power. You will create the best impact by speaking on the outward breath, by using the diaphragm – the muscle that can best be described as the "kicker", and which propels the breath and the voice outwards. Only in this way can an actor use their voice to fill a large theatre and it also helps control nerves. If the technique will cope with that then no presenter should have a great problem.

It is easy to demonstrate this to yourself. If you receive a shock, you automatically breathe in sharply by contracting the diaphragm, then "hold" the breath without letting go. Try it. Take a sharp breath. Hold it. You will find that some tension soon starts to creep in. Now breathe

87

out with a big, audible sigh. The diaphragm relaxes and the tension vanishes. Often everyday speech happens on the held breath, and the breath is only released after complete a sentence.

The best way to project is to speak during the exhalation of a breath. Try it. Notice the difference. Proper breathing – in slowly through the mouth, expanding the rib cage front, back and sides – imagine the rib cage is like a bellows – is the only way to obtain sufficient air when speaking. It fills the lungs fully and easily. And fast. Taking a few slow, deep breaths like this before you start a talk, particularly if you consciously relax the shoulders and chest as you do so, will relax you.

With this working well you can concentrate on using your voice to produce the modulation and the emphasis any formal presentation needs. Certain potential problems can be cured simply by the manner in which you speak. For example, a person who habitually speaks too fast has only to articulate words (and especially consonants) and pronounce the endings of words clearly, and the pace slows automatically.

All good advice and there is one additional comment: men and women have voices of different pitch. A woman whose voice is strained will start to sound squeaky if she forces it. Some women need intentionally to pitch their voice just a little lower than they would in normal conversation. The voice is the vehicle for your messages. To attempt to make presentations with no conscious thought of it is a bit like setting out on a long car journey without checking the petrol gauge, seeing if the tyres are inflated or looking at a map.

Finally, all that has been said in this chapter links back to preparation. Perhaps the greatest antidote to any sign of nerves is to know you are thoroughly and well prepared. You know what you are going to talk about (and what you will omit), how you are going to go through the message – in detail, the order, where you will exemplify, illustrate or give emphasis. You have related this to the audience to whom you will speak. You have worked out the timing and have made suitable notes which are in front of you.

Then as you rise to your feet instead of thinking, *I hope this will be all right*, you can say to yourself (and mean it), *I believe this is going to go well*. Having done your homework your confidence will rise and outweigh your uncertainties.

By organising things along the lines suggested, you effectively reduce the number of things on which your mind has to focus to manageable proportions. You can then concentrate solely on what you say and how you deliver it. Realistically there may be some other things to be borne in mind, but they can be kept firmly on the sidelines.

Remember, you may (presently) be unaccustomed to public speaking – but you should never be unprepared.

DURING THE PRESENTATION

Chapter Six
Involving your listeners

'I do not object to people looking at their watches when I am speaking. But I strongly object when they start shaking them to make certain they are still working.'
Lord Birkett (British Circuit Judge) 1883 – 1962

You cannot just speak. Any kind of public speech is, in part, visual. It is a truism about the way people take in information that seeing as well as hearing makes getting and maintaining attention more likely. This means that, if circumstances allow, then it is a good idea to have something visual alongside what you say.

Perhaps the most important visual aid has already been mention – you. Numbers of factors, such as simple gestures (for example, a hand pointing), and more dramatic ones like banging a fist on the table, which I like to describe as flourishes, are part of this, as is your general manner and appearance.

But all sorts of things can be used as visual aids. A picture is said to be worth a thousand words. Certainly a picture can largely speak for itself, and it may be in many forms: a painting, a photograph (black and white or colour), a line drawing or cartoon. A well chosen illustration can make an otherwise bland point memorable. Remember that many such things, published in a magazine say, are under copyright and should not be used publicly without permission.

Items can be produced from a pocket (money); larger things from below the table or behind a lectern (a bottle of wine); or even unveiled rather as at an official ceremony (like a sheet being pulled from over a life-sized cardboard cut-out photograph of a person). Anything like this can work well, and, of course, it works best when it has real relevance and is not just "clever".

But more traditional forms of visual aid are also important. Such things as PowerPoint slides serve several roles; these include:

- Focusing attention within the group.
- Helping change pace, add variety and so on.
- Giving a literally visual aspect to something.
- Acting as signposts to where within the structure the presentation has reached.

This helps you keep track, providing reminders over and above your speaker's notes on what comes next.

Be careful. Visual aids should *support* the message, not lead or take it over. Just because PowerPoint exists and is now almost universally used, does not mean it is always right. You need to start by looking at the message, at what you are trying to do, and see what will help put it over and have an additive effect. They may make a point that is difficult or impossible to describe, in the way a graph might make an instant point which might otherwise be lost in a mass of figures.

As an example here, the simple pie chart in the figure below, makes a clear point about the need to think about how much of a presentation comes over to the audience through the visuals and how much through the person doing the presenting. This may also make a useful image to keep in mind as you prepare and then give talks.

Whatever your reasons for using visual aids, make sure you use them appropriately. You may have a particular reason to use them: to help get a large amount of information over more quickly, perhaps. Or to illustrate a serious point (say in the construction industry context) more lightly by way of quoting an amusing newspaper headline: "*Bridge held up by red tape*". It needs to be just right.

Use of visual aids

The checklist that follows deals, briefly, with the various options, offers general guidance on the production and use of visual aids, and some tips on using the ubiquitous Overhead Projector (OHP) and PowerPoint. A further checklist at the end of this chapter sets out and compares the advantages and disadvantages of the main methods.

❑   Keep the content simple.
❑   Restrict the amount of information and the number of words:
    – Use single words to give structure, headings, or short statements
    – Avoid a cluttered, fussy or complicated look
    – Use a running logo (like a main heading/ topic on each slide)

[Without a doubt the worst, and commonest, fault in using visual aids is to pack them so full of information as to make them more confusing than illuminating. More of this anon.]

❑   Use diagrams, graphs and the like where possible rather than too many numbers; and never read figures aloud without visual support.
❑   Build in variety within the overall theme: for example, with colour or variations of the form of aid used.
❑   Emphasise the theme and structure: for example, regularly using a single aid to recap the agenda or objectives.
❑   Ensure the content of the visual matches the words you will use (so, for example, do not put the word logistics on a slide and then talk only about timing – it leaves people unsure quite where you are).
❑   Make certain all content is necessary and relevant (a common fault is the use of existing items – a graph or page from a report,

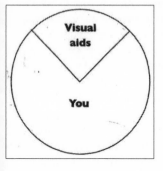

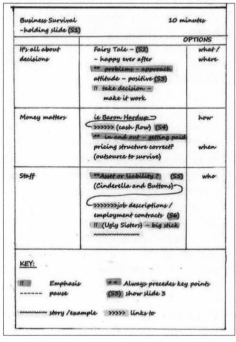

perhaps – and then ignoring most of what is there, focusing on one aspect of it only. People can see the rest, however, and part of their mind is distracted wondering what it is all about).

❑ Confirm that everything is visible: asking someone to help if you can't do it yourself: Is it clear? Is it bright enough? Is there sufficient contrast? Will it work in the room? Does it suit the equipment? (Colours, and the right sized typeface help here.)

❑ Check that the layout emphasises the meaning you want (and not some minor detail).

❑ Pick the right aid for the right purpose.

Using any sort of visual aid needs a little orchestrating. It can be awkward initially to have to speak, keep your place, remember to show something and actually organise to do so. The answer is easy:

take a moment and do not allow the process to rattle you. If people cannot see what you are doing, and frankly even if they can, just bridge any slight gap in the content of what you are saying with a descriptive comment – "The next slide illustrates this; let me just show you". In the time you take to say even that much, what you have to do will likely be done.

More than one US President has been accused of being unable to think and chew gum at the same time. But if you prefer to keep silent for a moment, let us say as you write something up on a flip chart, or an OHP, so be it. No one will mind, especially if it is preceded by a brief comment of explanation. Saying one thing and writing something else simultaneously is complicated. It is much better to take a moment to get it right than try to do two things at once and stumble.

The two most commonly used ways of projecting slides are the OHP and PowerPoint. The latter is now universally more popular. There are other things, of course, such as 35mm slides (though that changes the feel of a presentation as the lights need turning down for people to see them and any visual elements projected by the speaker disappear). But to be thorough, we will take these in turn.

Using an OHP
Some care should be taken in using an Overhead Projector to begin with. They may appear deceptively simple, but present inherent hazards to the unwary. The following hints may well be useful:

- Make sure the cable is out of the way (or taped to the floor); falling over it will improve neither your presentation nor your dignity.
- Check that it works before you start using it with the group (this goes for the second bulb – and a spare, even – and the roll of acetate film if you are using one).
- Ensure it is positioned where you want; within reach, and giving you room to move and space alongside for papers (note: it may need to be in a slightly different place for left/right-handed people – a hazard for some team presentations).
- Stand back and to the side of it: be sure not to obscure the view of the screen for anyone in the group.

- Having made sure the picture is in focus, look primarily at the machine and not the screen – the OHP's primary advantage is to keep you facing the front.
- Only use slides that have big enough typefaces or images. If you plan to write on acetate, check how large your handwriting needs to be.
- Switch off when changing slides; it looks more professional than the jumbled image that appears as slides are changed while the unit is on.
- If you want to project the image on a slide progressively you can cover the bottom part of the image with a sheet on paper (placed over the slide on the machine). Use paper that is not too thick and you will still be able to see the whole image through it even though the whole image is not projected. As you slide the paper down it may be useful to put a weight on it, otherwise it reaches the point where it must be held or will drop off.
- For hand-written notes, using an acetate roll, fitted running from the back to the front of the machine, minimising the amount of acetate used (it is expensive), removes the need to keep changing loose sheets. Things can be written as you go, or ahead of starting; if you need to draw something like a circle, then this might sensibly be done ahead to ensure it is neat.
- Remember that when something new is shown, all attention is, at least momentarily, on it – so always pause for a moment as something is revealed, or what you say may be missed.
- It may be useful to add emphasis by highlighting certain things on the slides as you go through them; if you slip the slide *under* the acetate roll you can do this without adjustment and without marking the slide.
- Similarly, two slides shown together can add information (or you can use overlays attached to the slide and folded across); alternatively, the second slide may have minimal information on it, with such things as a title talk, session heading, or company logo remaining in view as others are shown by being placed over it.
- If you want to point something out and highlight it, then this is most easily done by laying a small pointer (or pencil) on the

projector. Extending pointers are, in my view, almost impossible to use without appearing pretentious, and they risk you turning your back on the group unnecessarily.

OHP is still some people's preferred option despite PowerPoint's rapid growth in popularity.

PowerPoint

This allows you to prepare slides on your computer and show them through a projector via a computer, with which you control the show. It works well and you have the ability to use a variety of layouts, colours, illustrations and so on at the touch of a button.

There are some dangers (and many of the points made in reviewing the use of an OHP apply equally here). First, do not let the technology carry you away. Not everything it will do is useful – certainly not all on one slide or even in one presentation. It is a common enough error to allow the ease of preparation to increase the amount of information on a slide to a point where it is difficult to follow. This can lead to using too many slides. Similarly, if you are going to use its various features, like the ability to strip in one line and then another to make up a full picture, remember to keep whatever is done manageable. Details here can be important, for instance colour choice is prodigious but not all are equally suitable for making things clear.

The second danger is simply the increased risk of technological complexity. Sometimes this produces a simple error. Recently I saw an important presentation have to proceed without the planned slides because the projector (resident at the venue) could not be connected to the laptop computer (which had been brought to the venue) because the leads were incompatible. Sometimes problems may be caused by something buried in the software.

Again not long ago, I sat through a presentation that used 20 or 30 slides, and each time the slide was changed there was an unplanned delay of three or four seconds. It was felt unwarranted to stop and risk tinkering with the equipment, but long before the three-quarters of an hour presentation finished everyone in the group found it disproportionately maddening.

So make sure (check, check, check ...) that everything is going to work. Run off transparencies that can be shown on an OHP in the event of disaster striking if this would be a sensible insurance (or a paper handout copy). Finally, follow all the overall rules and remember that you do not have to have a slide on all the time. When you have finished with one, blank out the screen until you are ready for the next slide. [Just press the B key, and continue by pressing it again.]

Whatever you use, remember to talk to the group – not to the visual aid. Looking over your shoulder at the screen too much when slides are used is a common fault. Make sure visuals are visible, but do not get in the way yourself. Explain them or their purpose as necessary; mention whether or not people will get a paper copy of them at the end of the talk. Stop slides from distracting by removing them/turning screen blank as soon as you are finished with them.

Beware gremlins
Is it one of Murphy's Laws? Certainly it is an accurate maxim that if something can go wrong it will; and nowhere is this truer than with electrical and I.T. equipment.

The moral: check, check and check again. Everything – including what leads the more sophisticated equipment needs to make it work. Carry a spare copy of your presentation on a memory stick in case the laptop fails to spring into life. Even whether the pens for the flip chart still work is worth checking.

Always double-check anything with which you are unfamiliar. If a microphone is going to be essential, you should do a sound check,. And remember that while the sophistication of equipment increases all the time, so too do the number of things that can potentially go wrong.

The concept of contingency is worth a thought; what do you do if disaster does strike? You have been warned.

The dangers of standardisation
The use of PowerPoint is now ubiquitous. The system is in almost every computer. Literally tens of millions of people use it – and do so around the globe. It makes creating simple slides easy, but it also standardises to a worrying extent.

Imagine: He who must be listened to stands at the front of the room, surrounded by equipment and with the screen glowing behind him. The audience is spellbound. The little company logo at the corner of the screen fascinates them. Every time the presenter clicks the computer mouse and sends another yellow bullet point shuttling onto the screen from stage left, their attention soars. One slide replaces another, then another replaces that and another ... but you get the idea. Enough.

All are bland, all are simple checklists, yet he who must be listened to finds them riveting. Certainly he spends most of his time looking over his shoulder at the screen rather than at the audience.

There is so much text on some slides that they are like pages out of a book. And an unsuitably small typeface compounds the effect and overburdens the minds of the audience. The figure that follows shows this standardisation graphically.

So he reads them, verbatim, more slowly than the audience does and with a tone that leads one to suspect that he is seeing them for the first time.

It becomes akin to a bureaucratic rain dance: a mantra and format is slavishly, indeed unthinkingly, followed – yet at the end no one is truly satisfied. The opportunity – the open goal – is missed.

EXAMPLE SLIDE

The main heading

- This is a bullet point
- This is another
- This is another
- This is one more
- And this is yet another
- And this is a bullet point as well
- And this ... you get the idea

If only good business presentations were that easy, so mechanistic. Put up one slide, read everything crammed onto it out loud, repeat slide by slide, and success follows automatically. But they are not. Large numbers of lack lustre, wordy slides do not make a good presentation. Certainly they do not make a distinctive or memorable one. But then perhaps, honestly assessed, he who must be listened to did not really believe they did.

The slides are there – be honest – because that is how presentations are prepared. A ubiquitous norm is followed largely unthinkingly, and the results fail to sparkle. Indeed they may fail to explain, inform and certainly to persuade.

It is worth suggesting care too with the equally universal ClipArt. Again this is on most computers and allows you to select little illustrations and slot them into the corner of a slide, which would otherwise show only words. Too often the illustrations chosen only add a modicum of something visual. They are trite, only loosely linked to the text and add little or nothing to the totality of the slide they adorn. They are picked out as a routine and little thought is involved.

Audiences may put up with all this, and a comparison with the norm of their experience may not be so bad, but everyone is aware that something is missing.

Signs of revolt
Such a by-the-book approach, screening out any real, individual consideration of what is best, is so prevalent among PowerPoint users and so ill-thought of by those on the receiving end of such presentations that it has become subject of academic and journalistic comment. They have even coined the phrase: *Death by PowerPoint*.. And it is the slides used that come in for the greatest criticism.

For instance, in America a well-known and respected academic, Edward R Tufte of Yale, who is a communications expert, has written a strong condemnation of PowerPoint, in his article *"The Cognitive Style of PowerPoint"* (which you can read in full by accessing www.edwardtufte.com). One fascinating example he uses concerns the Columbia space shuttle disaster. In a slide presentation, which Tufte calls, *an exercise in misdirection*, a crucial piece of information in which the foam section that detached and crippled the craft is described as 640 times larger than ones which reassuring pre-flight advice described, was buried in small type several layers down in a packed PowerPoint list. Though the danger was actually flagged, the warning it gave was not noticed. The main heading on the slide indicated a positive outcome to tests, saying: "Review of Test Data indicates Conservatism for Tile Penetration". One might criticise the language too, but the point remains – the key information was passed over unnoticed.

To reinforce any lingering feeling that traditional PowerPoint style and practice are fine, try looking at www.norvig.com/Gettysburg where Peter Norvig has posted a wonderful spoof of Abraham Lincoln's Gettysburg address:

Four score and seven years ago our fathers brought forth on this continent a new nation, conceived in liberty and dedicated to the proposition that all men are created equal.

Such stirring language and thoughts are reduced to banality by a visual presentation that is not visual, and which uses bullet points such as *Met on battlefield (great)*. As an example of how to reduce a powerful and memorable message to insignificance; this is a classic.

In Britain, some years ago, a feature by John Naughton in the newspaper, *The Guardian*, addressed the same issue. He quoted Tufte's American article and added its own despairing spin: *Power corrupts. PowerPoint obfuscates. Next time you have to give a presentation, leave it at home.*

The reasons why such comment is made is obvious: the prevailing style of PowerPoint-driven presentations, while they are something audiences expect and tolerate, do not satisfy many audiences as they should. A good, stylish presenter, with presence and panache, may be able to make up for this – but only in part.

Go back to the essential rules set out above. Too much text is the worst mistake. It blights too many presentations, especially those made using PowerPoint. PowerPoint can do extraordinary things, buried in that seeming simple piece of software is a resource that can produce visuals that are striking, full of colour, movement and images and which truly deserve the term "visual aid".

That said, the intention is not to put you off using PowerPoint, or indeed any other similar system. It is intended as a warning, and to emphasise the need for some thought about it. In particular to flag the danger of doing any of this as a routine – working, if you like, on automatic pilot.

As a dramatic example of the way in which the automatic pilot operates – the rut it can put you in is a deep one – consider the following example. [This is taken from a book *Marketing and Selling Professional Services,* written by Patrick Forsyth, published by Kogan Page]. It concerns a sales pitch for which the firm of architects involved prepared slides to show to the committee of a charity for the blind. They really did not think of the audience – but just blindly (I know) followed the routine of how their presentations were always prepared.

They based it on a battery of slides and pictures. The absurdity of it only dawned on them minutes before the presentation was due to start. They found that 10 of the 12 strong committee were blind. As the Managing Director of the firm reflected afterwards: *If that can be overlooked, anything can be overlooked.*

This may seem fantastic but it really happened and provides testimony to the power – and danger – of operating on automatic pilot. Do not just sail unthinkingly into some preordained way of preparing something. The same complacency can affect all manner of other, if lesser, disasters or mishaps.

Anything and everything

Finally, it pays to adopt an inventive approach here. As has been said, practically anything can act as a visual aid, from another person (carefully briefed to play their part) to an exhibit of some sort. In a business presentation, exhibits may be obvious items: products, samples, posters etc, or may be something totally unexpected.

Something unexpected, surprising or striking can have considerable impact. The owner of a kitchen equipment company was giving a demonstration of his latest range of cookers. Everyone in the audience found a complimentary pair of oven gloves on their seat.

Conversely, if something complicated is necessary, then it may work best as a handout. Each delegate can look at their personal copy, take in the detail and then relate it to what is being said.

Like all the skills involved in making presentations, while the basics give you a sound foundation, the process is something that can benefit from a little imagination.

Now, a useful checklist before we move on.

CHECKLIST

Different methods of visualisation compared

Flip charts
Advantages

- [ ] No power source needed.
- [ ] Can be prepared beforehand.
- [ ] Can be adapted/amended as you go.
- [ ] Easy to see.
- [ ] Available at many venues.
- [ ] Easy to write on (use sufficiently large writing).
- [ ] Can use different colours.
- [ ] You can refer back and forward.

Disadvantages

- [ ] Expensive to prepare professionally.
- [ ] Large and awkward to move.
- [ ] Masking is difficult/messy.
- [ ] Poor handwriting spoils effect.

Overall: makes a better work pad than a means of presenting prepared information.

Fixed white board
Advantages

- [ ] Available at many venues.

- ❏ Useful work pad.
- ❏ If metal backed will allow magnets to hold paper.

Disadvantages

- ❏ Needs special pens. (Be careful! A venue will not be pleased if you use permanent pens on one.)
- ❏ Poor handwriting can spoil effect.
- ❏ Erasing takes longer than turning a page on a flip chart.

Overall: another good work pad.

OHP
Advantages

- ❏ Can be seen in a brightly lit room.
- ❏ Produces a large image.
- ❏ Masking is easily possible (allowing a message to be revealed progressively).
- ❏ Slides can be prepared, reused and are easily transported.
- ❏ Look professional.
- ❏ Available at many venues.
- ❏ Slides act as prompts (and information on frames can be visible to the speaker but not to the audience).

Disadvantages

- ❏ Needs a power source.
- ❏ Can be noisy (fan).
- ❏ A little obtrusive standing between the speak and audience.
- ❏ Can break down.
- ❏ Requires a screen or suitable wall to project onto.
- ❏ Needs getting used to if speaker is to appear professional.

Overall: good as a prepared base for slides, but with acetate sheets or roll can act as a work pad as well. Can project pictures, maybe not as well as 35mm slide projector, but does so without having to have the room darkened, something that rules out 35mm slides for many uses as the speaker effectively disappears.

PowerPoint

Advantages

- ❑ Universally used.
- ❑ Full use of the software can produce awesome images.
- ❑ Normally all is well, but use needs care, preparation and some people feel safest with back up. For example, slides also printed off ready to run on an OHP in case a problem develops.

Disadvantages

- ❑ Origination takes time.
- ❑ May need training and can be very expensive if done professionally.
- ❑ The chances of something going wrong increase as the technology is complex.

Overall: the methodology of choice for so many things; anyone speaking regularly at events probably needs some familiarity with this.

Handouts
Advantages

- ❑ Can look professional.
- ❑ Allows specific detailed points to be looked at.
- ❑ Good for technical information.

Disadvantages

- ❑ Temptation to use too much information.
- ❑ Can distract more easily from verbal presentation (and cannot be easily removed after use).

Overall: has its place for certain types of information. May also distract as they are distributed

Next, we consider other ways of involving your audience.

AFTER THE PRESENTATION

Chapter Seven
Question time and feedback

'The best audience is intelligent, well educated and a little drunk.'
Alben W Barkley

The last chapter covered the use of equipment and visual aids and how to involve the audience. As has been stressed throughout, audiences are important; but they should never be regarded simply as a passive target. They may sometimes need – or demand – to be involved. Certainly there should always be a link with them. Eye contact has been mentioned earlier. The feedback that comes from it and from general observation of the sound and signs of the group and from individual members of it are always going to underpin any involvement with the audience.

In small groups, presentations may sometimes be only a step removed from a round table meeting. A manager at the head of a boardroom table, or the Chair of a committee, may be on their feet and presenting, yet still engage members of the group in individual exchanges – to obtain more pointed and immediate feedback perhaps: "What is your view of this, Mary?" Too far in this direction takes us into training or perhaps counselling, rather than presentation or speech making. Here, in the context of formal presentations, involvement is taken to mean the process of encouraging, where that is necessary or desirable, and dealing with, questions.

So, how do we tackle this issue? In three stages, considering: *when* to take questions, *how to prompt them* when desired and then *how to answer* them.

When to take questions

The first thing to be said here is that the option to decide when to take questions may not be in the control of the speaker. If an invitation to speak is issued, then the format of the meeting may well be fixed. This is as likely to be the case both internally (within an organisation) or externally to an outside group.

Always find out, well before you speak, what the format of a particular meeting is. If you think some variant would be better (either for you or for the meeting) *consider* asking whoever is in charge if the format might be adjusted. Be careful: if you demand your own way in some situations it may do you no good at all. You may be better to live with, and make the best of, the planned or routine arrangements. Indeed you may have no choice whatsoever due to the location or venue. Different situations demand different approaches, and sometimes a specific suggestion will be welcomed.

Broadly the options are:

- To take questions at any time throughout the presentation. This should only be done if you are able, and willing, to keep control as it can prove disruptive – certainly to time-keeping. Also, you must be sure you are going to cope well with the questions. An early one, say, that gets you flustered can dent the most promising of starts.
- Taking questions at the end of the session. This can frustrate the audience and may give you a false sense of security. While you speak uninterrupted, you can think that everything you are saying is being completely accepted.
- A mix of both. Perhaps a main question session at the end, but one or two others encouraged or allowed on the way through. These can be prompted at moments when the talk will benefit from some interaction or feedback.
- No questions at any time. A formal session may be followed by something else that does facilitate questions. Such an example

might include an informal chat between members of the audience over some form of refreshments afterwards.

Most presentations will be followed by questions. Indeed you may wish to prompt them to create discussion or debate, or simply to avoid an embarrassing gap at the end of the session. One important point is relevant here. You will often do best to keep the last word of the whole session for yourself. A common danger of a question session is that it tails away at the end and thus, especially if someone else is in the Chair, the final word is taken away from you.

What can happen is that, after a few questions, they are slower coming, the last one is somewhat insubstantial, perhaps, and the Chair ends the meeting: "Well there seem to be no more questions; let's leave it there and thank our speaker …".

A better route can be to introduce question time in a way that reserves the right to the speaker of the final word. This can be done even through the Chair: "Right, Mr Chairman, perhaps we should see if there are any questions. Then perhaps I could reserve two minutes to summarise before we close". Few people taking the Chair will take exception to that, still less so if everything is going well.

Directing questions
Sometimes you need to prompt comments and questions, as perhaps at a committee meeting. There are formal inputs, but you also – especially if you are in the chair – may want to canvass opinion. There are several ways of directing questions you can use:

- *Overhead questions:* that is questions put to the group generally, and useful for opening up a subject. If there is no response, then you can move on to the next method. "Right, what do you think the key issue here is? Anyone?"
- *Overhead and then directed at an individual:* this method is useful to make the whole group think before looking for an answer from one person: "Right, what do you think the key issues here are? Anyone? …John, what do you think?"
- *Direct to individual:* this is useful for obtaining individual responses, and testing for understanding: "John, what do you think …?"

- *Non-response/rhetorical questions:* this is useful where you want to make a point to one or more persons in the group without concentrating on anyone in particular, or for raising a question you would expect to be in the group's mind and then answering it yourself: "What's the key issue? Well, perhaps it's ..."

All these methods represent very controlled discussion: dialogue that goes from speaker to group member to speaker and then to another group member (or more), and finally ... back to the speaker.

In addition, bear in mind these two types of question, the use of which can help to open up a discussion:

- *Re-directed questions.* These are useful to prompt discussion and involvement in the group and answer questions posed to you: "That's a good point John. What do you think the answer is, Mary?" This makes people think and creates involvement, rather than simply providing an answer by the speaker directed at one individual.
- *Developmental questioning.* Here you take the answer to a previous question and move it around the audience, building on it and asking further questions: "Having established that, how about ...?"

Whichever of the above is being used, and this depends primarily on the relative importance of the topic raised, certain principles should be borne in mind. When you use questions to create involvement, then for what you do to be effective, the following general method may be a useful guide to the kind of sequence that can be employed:

- *State the question clearly and concisely.* Questions should relate directly to the subject being discussed. Whenever possible they should require people to think, to draw on their past experiences, and relate them to the present circumstances.
- *Ask the question first to the group rather than to an individual.* If the question is directed to a single individual, others are off the hook and do not have think about the answer. Direct, individual questions are more useful to break a general silence in the group, or to involve someone who is not actively participating in the

discussion and who you want to draw in.

- *After asking the question ... pause*. Allow a few moments for the group to consider what the answer should be; do not be tempted to rush on, embarrassed by the silence, and provide an answer in a way that curtails any involvement. Then, if silence continues:
- *Ask a specific individual to answer* (and give them a moment to think too). This four-step process starts the entire group thinking because they never know who will be called on. Thus everyone has to consider each question you ask and be ready to participate. Even those who are not called on are still involved.

To be sure of using an effective questioning technique, there are some things which should be avoided, such as:

- *Asking yes or no questions*. Participants can attempt to guess the answer (and may be right). These questions should not be used if you want participants to use their reasoning power and actively participate.
- *Asking unanswerable questions*. You want to provide information, not confusion. Be sure that the knowledge and experience of your group are such that at least some participants can answer any questions you are asking. Never attempt to highlight ignorance by asking questions which the group cannot handle. And this is particularly true when you are trying to draw out a silent participant and involve them. Be sure they can answer before you ask them the questions. Though, incidentally, there is another kind of unanswerable question, posed rhetorically, simply for humorous effect. Such include the likes of: *Why is abbreviated such a long word? Why is a boxing ring square? Why does the partner who snores always go to sleep first? What does occasional furniture do the rest of the time?* And many more no doubt, providing another way of injecting a brief light touch.
- *Asking personal questions*. Personal questions are usually rather sensitive, even in one-to-one sessions. They are often inappropriate in a group session. Though again there can be exceptions, which then make an impact. I sometimes ask a group member, *Are you married?* And always get a sort of double take –

this is in the context of talking about avoiding bland language. "If I said your wife/husband was 'quite nice', you are entitled to be upset; they are surely far more than that ..."

- *Asking leading questions.* By leading questions, I mean ones in which the speaker indicates the preferred answer in advance: "Mary, don't you agree that this new form will help solve the problem?" Such questions require little effort on the part of the participant and will often just annoy. In addition, even if Mary did not agree, she would probably be uncomfortable saying so, given that rejection is apparently not being invited. It is especially important not to lead in this way if you are the most senior person present in an organisational setting.

- *Repeating questions.* Do not make a practice of repeating the question for an inattentive person. Doing so simply encourages further inattention and wastes valuable time. Instead, ask someone else to respond. People will quickly learn that they have to listen. This is especially useful in something like a committee situation – did you ever attend a committee meeting that finished early?

- *Allowing group answers.* Unless written down (and then referred to around the group), questions that allow several members of the group to answer are not particularly useful. First, everyone cannot talk at once. Second, with group answers a few participants may well tend to dominate the session. And third, group answers allow the silent person to hide and not participate as they should

Note: the two invaluable and unbreakable rules all sessions should have regarding participation and involvement, both being clearly understood and adhered to, are:

1. Only one person can talk at a time.
2. Whoever is in the Chair decides who that is.

Above all, in this area let your questioning be natural. Ask because you want to know – because you want this information to be shared with the group. Never think of yourself as a quizmaster, with certain questions that must be asked whether or not they are timely. Let your manner convey your interest in the response you are going to get and be sure that your interest is genuine. Forced, artificial enthusiasm will never fool a group.

In many situations none of these things may be necessary; all you have to do is answer questions that are put to you. So, let us think about how that can be done effectively.

Handling questions......
When questions do come, prompted, expected or otherwise, you need to think about how you answer them. The following suggested approach will help:

- Get the question right and never try to answer a point when you are actually not quite clear what is meant. If necessary ask for it to be repeated, check it back, "What you are asking is ... is that correct?" Make a quick written note of it if this helps.
- If the question was clear to you, but might not have been heard at the back of the room, that is behind the questioner, then either check this first or simply go straight to repeating it, saying it is for the benefit of others. Then, with the question clear, you can proceed to:
- Acknowledge the question and questioner: "Okay, Sue's asking for a comment about ..." Not least everything so far gives you a few moments to think, something that is often useful.
- Give short informative answers whenever possible and link to other parts of your message, as appropriate. If necessary it does no harm to say something like, "Right. Let me think about that for a moment". You cannot pause for long, but even an additional few seconds may help you get an answer straight in your mind; an audience expecting a considered response will not see this as unacceptable, maybe the reverse.

If you opt, which you may want to, for questions at any time, then remember that to keep things flowing it is perfectly acceptable to:

- Hold them for a moment until you finish making a point, "Good point, let me come to it in just a minute."
- Delay them; saying you will come back to it, in context, when you

get to a specific topic area. Then you must remember. Make a note of both the point and who made it.

- Refuse them. Some may be irrelevant or likely to lead to too much of a digression. Be *careful* not to do this too often, to respect the questioner's feelings, and to explain why you are doing so (maybe something is better handled later in another meeting, for instance).

- Say: "I don't know". If you don't know the answer, you *must* say so. You can offer to find out, you can see if anyone else in the group knows. You can certainly make a note of it for later. But if you attempt, unsuccessfully, to answer you will lose all credibility. No one, in fact, expects you to be omniscient, so do not worry about it. If you are well-prepared it will not happen often in any case.

A final dimension here is worth additional comment. Some "questions" (or statements) may be negative, contradictory – or both.

.....and objections

If your presentations are not contentious and are strictly one way, then objections may well be no problem. If, however, you actually do get objections voiced then they must be dealt with carefully. The first rule is to make sure you have the point made straight in your mind before you respond,. Remember the advice, quoted earlier, that it is best to engage the brain before the mouth.

There is nothing to say you cannot respond to a question with another question to clarify the query. Or repeat it back, varying the words: "What you are asking is ...Have I got that right?"

Similarly, you may want to delay an answer, and there is no reason why doing so cannot be made to sound perfectly acceptable: "That's certainly something I have to explain; perhaps I can pick it up, in context, when I get to ..." Objections can be delayed just as can any other kind of question.

It is wise also not to rush into an answer to an objection. Give it a moment (and yourself time to think). You may be amazed, and relieved, how much can go on in your mind even in a pause of just two or three seconds. A slight gap in proceedings is not a problem to the audience who may, in any case, expect you to consider the matter. Remember also that too glib an answer may be mistrusted, especially when one rushes straight in and starts, "Ah, but …". A pause gives the impression of consideration, respect for the questioner, and adds gravitas.

It may be just what is needed here. A pause plus an acknowledgement go well together, and also extend your private thinking time. It works well especially if the acknowledgement can be positive and make it clear you are not denying the point – or at least the relevance of it. Phrases like, "That's a good point" really can be appropriate. Better still, something that makes it clear that you are going to respond or explain further: "You're right. Cost is certainly a key issue. It is a great deal of money; let me say a word more about why I believe it is a good investment …" Remember the answer may need to make a point to the whole audience, rather than only to the individual who voiced doubts.

A final – important – point here. As has been said, never be afraid to say, "I don't know". You can offer to check a point later. You can ask if others in the group know, but the dangers of bluffing are all too apparent. You can end up having dug a very deep hole for yourself. However, do consider – in advance – what may come up.

A good many questions, and objections too for that matter, are surely wholly expected. You know, if you think about it, the kind of thing that is likely to be raised in a particular situation. Certainly it is no good identifying something as a possible problem and then doing nothing except hope that it will not materialise. You need to have answers in mind for matters that are likely to need dealing with; though realistically you must tailor them to particular circumstances.

Audiences are not, of course, entirely homogeneous groups. All sorts of people may be present. This affects the intentions of the speaker, as has already been intimated, but it also affects the handling of questions. Different people have different attitudes, motivations and manners and may put questions in many different ways.

The following section sets out some examples of types of questioner and something of the tactics suitable for dealing with each. Some are all too common, others you will rarely have to deal with, and still others only occur when question sessions slip into more open discussion.

Dealing with different styles of questioner

The "show-off"
Avoid embarrassing or shutting them off; you may need them later.
Solution: toss them a difficult question. Or say, "That's an interesting point. Let's see what the group thinks of it."

The "quick reactor"
Can also be valuable later, but can keep others out of the discussion.
Solution: thank them; suggest we take now also take questions from others.

The "heckler"
This one that argues about every point being made.
Solution: Remain calm. Agree, affirm any good points, but toss bad points to the group for discussion. They will be quickly rejected. Privately try to find out what it is that is bothering such a person, try to elicit their cooperation.

The "rambler"
Who talks about everything except the subject under discussion.
Solution: At a pause in their monologue, thank them, return to and restate relevant points of discussion and go on.

The "mutual enemies"
When there is a clash of personalities between members of the audience
Solution: Emphasise points of agreement, in a way that minimise differences. Or frankly ask that personalities be left out of things. Draw attention back to the point being made.

The "pig-headed"
A person who absolutely refuses, perhaps through prejudice, to accept points that are being discussed.
Solution: Throw their points to the group, have them straighten the person out. Mention that time is short, that you will be glad to discuss it with them later.

The "digresser"
Who takes the discussion too far off track.
Solution: Take the blame yourself. Say, "Something I said must have led you off the subject; this is what we should be discussing ..."

The "professional gripe"
Who makes clearly political points.
Solution: Politely point out that we cannot change policy here; the objective is to operate as best we can under the present system. Or better still, have a member of the group answer them.

The "whisperers"
Who hold private conversations, which, while they could be related to the subject, are distracting.
Solution: Do not embarrass them. Direct some point to one of them by name, ask an easy question. Or repeat the last point and ask for comments. Get them away from their separate conversation

The "inarticulate"
Who has the ideas, but cannot put them across.
Solution: Say, "Let me repeat that ..." (then put it in clearer language).

The "mistaken"
Who is clearly wrong.
Solution: Say, "That's one way of looking at it, but how can we reconcile that with ...?" (state the correct point).

The "silent"
Who could be shy, bored, indifferent, insecure, or who just might be taking things in and be listening carefully.
Solution: Depends on what I causing the silence. If the person is bored or indifferent, try asking a provocative question, one you think they might be interested in. If shy, compliment them when they *do* say something, and then ask them direct questions from time to time to draw them in.

In the Chair
This takes us outside the brief for this book. However, it is useful in the

context of question sessions to refer to it briefly. Indeed, some of what has been said in the last few pages is of most relevance if you *are* in the Chair. So, the checklist that follows reviews the whole question of chairmanship in any type of business or committee meeting where such a role is necessary.

CHECKLIST

Chairing/leading a meeting: guidelines for conducting the whole meeting (which might include presentation, discussion and debate, and questions).

The person directing the meeting must:

- ❑ command the respect of those attending;
- ❑ do their homework and come prepared, having read any relevant documents and taken any other action necessary to help them "take charge" . They should also encourage others to prepare – this makes for more considered and succinct contributions to the meeting and saves time;
- ❑ be punctual;
- ❑ start on time. It is also good practice to state an estimated a finishing time; people like to know how much time they are setting aside;
- ❑ ensure administrative matters will be taken care of correctly. This includes such things as refreshments, taking minutes, etc;
- ❑ start on the right note and lead into the agenda;
- ❑ introduce participants, if necessary. Certainly know who is who themselves – name cards can help at some kinds of meeting;
- ❑ set the rules;
- ❑ control the discussion, and the individual types present (the talkative, the quiet, the argumentative, and so on);
- ❑ encourage contributions where necessary;
- ❑ ask questions to clarify (this can be a great time saver);
- ❑ always query something unclear at once. If the meeting runs on when something has been misinterpreted it will take longer to sort

out and you will have to recap and re-cover a section);
- ❑ ensure everybody has their say;
- ❑ keep the discussion to the point;
- ❑ listen, as in listen. The leader should resolve any "But you said ..." arguments;
- ❑ watch the clock, and remind people of the time pressure ;
- ❑ summarise, clearly and succinctly, where necessary, which usually means regularly;
- ❑ ensure any necessary decisions are actually made, agreed and recorded;
- ❑ cope with any upsets, outbursts and emotion;
- ❑ provide the final word (summary) and bring matters to a conclusion (and link to any final administrative detail – things like setting another meeting date are often forgotten);
- ❑ see, afterwards, to any follow-up action (another great time-waster is people arriving at meetings not having taken action promised at a previous session);
- ❑ do all this with patience, goodwill, humour and respect for the various individuals present.

Being an effective chairperson is a skill that may warrant study and practice. A good chairperson is likely to be an effective speaker too. Certainly the two skills go together. Someone who is able to take the Chair, and execute the role competently, is a huge asset to any organisation.

One last point to end this chapter – the way a presentation is run and how the group is handled will have a considerable influence on how a question session goes. If the presentation is lacklustre, the audience's attention is not held. Indeed if the content – perhaps a contentious policy matter – has affected their mood, then any speaker will experience a hard time when questions are asked. Some members of the audience may want the speaker put on the spot and try to catch them out (and perhaps impress others). On the other hand, a speaker in control of the situation, of apparent expertise and authority, is always treated with a little more circumspection when it comes to question time.

So, prevention and cure is a good way of looking at this area. Failing all else, remember what Professor Roland Smith once said at a company

AGM: "I'll answer some of your questions. The more difficult ones will be answered by my colleagues."

Do your homework, know your stuff, do not be afraid to say, "I don't know" (although not *too* often!), and you will handle all the aspects of audience involvement and questions successfully. Won't you?

And finally......

> 'When you have nothing to say, say nothing.'
> *Charles Caleb Colton (1780 – 1832)*

Readers – (and to qualify for that description you have to have read your way through to this point, not flicked a page or two in from the back of the book) – at the end of this review of the process of presentation let me conclude by putting one or two matters in context and looking to the future.

There are essentially two aspects to what must be done to create, maintain and enhance your speaking skills. The first, assisted I hope by reading this book, is to have a sound appreciation of the techniques and processes that make a presentation go well. Knowledge of what works well provides the foundation from which you can work and expand your capabilities.

Secondly, you need practice. This can come from attending a course, and – if that involves using video (recording what participants do) – not only having a chance to see how you come over, but to discuss the detail of this with other members of the group and with the tutor. A course will also allow you quickly to see other examples of the kinds of things that have to be tackled in a variety of different presentational situations. Or, of course, you can gain experience from actually making real presentations, and the idea of actively seeking out opportunities to accelerate that experience was mentioned in the text.

Presentation is a skill where the process of adding usefully to your experience is, you will find, never ending. There are a number of ways in which you can continue to acquire knowledge about the techniques:

- Reading additional books and other references on the topic.

- Seeing training films on the subject.
- Meeting and discussing with colleagues (especially to plan or review actual future talks or run construction post-mortems on past ones).
- Rehearsing in front of, and with, colleagues and noting comments before going on to a final version (so pick a colleague with no reason to flatter you).
- Reviewing what you do and aiming to learn from experience: for instance noting things to not do, work on or use again.

All this means there is certainly opportunity to extend learning and practice. Make no mistake, whatever you may have done already, presentational skill cannot have too much practice. To do this effectively you must remain objective and be prepared to analyse honestly what you do (and take on board any feedback from others). Then you can ensure your techniques will improve continually. Within an organisation it may help to improve skills if people are:

- Encouraged to rehearse what they have to do.
- Encouraged also to seek out additional chances to increase practice opportunities (some companies run internal talks, make certain internal meetings more formal than might otherwise be necessary, and take other similar actions to provide such occasions).

Depending on your position this may be a process with which you can play a part, encouraging members of your staff if you are a manager, for instance. On a personal scale, even if you are just on one committee but know that your role could well involve more formal speaking situations, it is worthwhile to look for ways to practice ahead of more important occasions.

The rewards in corporate and career terms, and in a social context too, of developing good presentational skills are considerable. What is more, good habits do set in, a process that is more likely if you set out to make it so. If you develop the habit of thorough preparation and develop good habits regarding exactly how you go about it, then you will find your whole approach will ease the end result.

A good system for preparing your notes will prompt you to ask yourself if there should be a visual aid at certain points. It will raise the query whether there are sufficient of them overall, and how to do this more certainly and effectively. Good and sufficient visual aids will, in turn, augment the presentation. The thinking and the process create a positive loop.

Moreover, practice, will soon begin to take some of the chore out of the whole process. Preparation does not take so long for those who know how to go about it and who have a good system for doing it. Even seemingly awkward factors, such as judging how long a message will take to run through, become more certain with practice.

Beyond all this, to a degree, the sky is the limit. The best presenters make it look very easy, though this may simply disguise careful preparation, rehearsal and execution. Training, study and simply practice and sensible consideration of how you have done can help everyone move towards an acceptable standard. But it can do more than this. Charisma, often regarded (indeed defined) as a gift, actually consists (certainly in part) of intentionally applied techniques.

Good eye contact, appropriate verbal emphasis, a careful choice of words and gestures, the confidence to hold a pause – and more – all cumulatively add to personal appeal. Such techniques can be learned, developed and deployed to enhance the overall effect. Someone who has the ability to generate genuine enthusiasm is naturally charismatic. For the rest, in many ways it adds up to a respect for the audience and the occasion.

The last thing people want is to sit through a lacklustre presentation. Those who work hard at how they do it and use the available techniques appropriately allow their personality to shine through. These people make the best job of it, and this helps both the audience and themselves. The alternative, a dreary presentation and an audience who resent it, is not a happy one.

Thank you for reading this far. I hope you will find that the content of this book will act as a catalyst, giving you some ideas both to implement and deploy immediately and others to work on and adapt. The rest is up to you. You are the only coach who is always there when you get up to speak.

If you have already had some practice, consider what you are doing against the knowledge of the principles set out here. This will help you achieve an even higher standard. If you are nervously awaiting your first outing: go for it. You now know something of the techniques involved and how they can assist with building your confidence. Aim to surprise yourself, and your audience. You may just find that it is fun.

CHECKLIST

Presentation performance
You can prompt a great deal of change and improvement when needed simply by analysing what you do. The list that follows is arranged under four main areas:

- Content
- Structure
- Manner
- Maintenance of interest

If things go well under all these headings then there is every chance something will appeal to the audience. You can mark yourself for all those factors listed and resolve if necessary to work at any areas you consider need change.

Content: what you said

- ❑ Clear and understandable
- ❑ Level of detail
- ❑ Level of technicality
- ❑ Logical sequence
- ❑ Evidence or proof
- ❑ Link to visual aids/documentation
- ❑ Relevance to the audience

Structure: arrangement of content

❑ Clear purpose
❑ Overall direction
❑ Use of signposting
❑ The Beginning: an effective start/statement of intent
❑ The Middle: a logical progression
❑ The End: summary/loose ends/request for action/high note
❑ Continuity
❑ Timing

Manner: impression made

❑ Personal appearance
❑ Stance
❑ Use of gestures
❑ Projection
❑ Rapport
❑ Empathy
❑ Pace
❑ Eye contact
❑ Voice: variety and emphasis
❑ Management of the speaking environment
❑ Coping with the unexpected
❑ Sensitivity

Maintenance of interest: appeal to audience

❑ Focus on audience
❑ Enthusiasm
❑ Use of examples
❑ Illustration
❑ Humour
❑ Aids: appropriate method/clear images/match what was said/ illustrative
❑ Management of any necessary audience involvement
❑ Adding "Flourish"
❑ Overall animation

You can mark yourself in various ways: a good way is to use four levels of comment. These can be A, B, C, and D if you like, or you can give them descriptions such as: Satisfactory/Above Average/Below Average/ Unsatisfactory. By using an even number of ratings you cannot mark yourself "aAverage". If you are mostly marked in the top two ratings, this would indicate all is well for the moment. However, the lower two would suggest that some sort of action or change needs to take place. In this way it is easier to finetune what you do and make sure that you gradually improve your performance as you discover how things are working out.

Acknowledgements

I am able to write books on business topics – and presentations in particular – only because of the help I have received from others along the way. A number of people have prompted and encouraged me towards public speaking in the past. I have listened to many others over the years and learned something every time I have been in the audience (even if it is what not to do...).

Thanks are also due to the many people I have met in the course of my consulting and training work – and the many colleagues I have worked with, conversations I have had and questions I have asked both in public and corporate seminars. Any such events I have attended have added to my knowledge and experience of how things work in this area. Thank you all.

Finally, writing – and the process that goes with it of getting published – is, for the most part, a solitary process. Collaboration with other writers can be both useful and enjoyable. In this context I would like to thank Patrick Forsyth, always an admirable collaborator, and who assisted in getting this particular work of the ground.

Frances Kay

Frances Kay

With many years work experience, covering politics, diplomatic service and law, Frances has helped professional individuals and organisations on all aspects of career and personal development, and relationship building. The majority of her time is now spent writing business books and articles, researching, editing and giving interviews, talks and workshops on her book topics.

Five years ago Kogan Page Publishers appointed Frances Kay Editor of their bestselling title *The Good Non Retirement Guide*, an annual publication. The 26th edition appears in January 2012. The book covers every aspect of retirement, from managing money, health, property, making the most of your leisure to starting and running your own business.

Since turning 60 herself, Frances has relished the challenges and opportunities that this project has involved. Frances also spends time helping entrepreneurs and small businesses on a pro-bono basis – particularly those located in Gloucestershire.

Other Books in Smart Skills Series

Mastering the Numbers

Meetings

Negotiation

Persuasion

Working with Others

www.smartskillsbooks.com

www.legendpress.co.uk

www.twitter.com/legend_press